OFF NEVSKY PROSPEKT

LIFE AMONG LENINGRAD'S UNOFFICIAL ARTISTS

BARBARA J. HAZARD

Cover painting by Elena Figurina

All photos by Barbara J. Hazard except for those indicated

All chapter drawings by Barbara J. Hazard

Cover and interior by Charles Fuhrman Design

Typography by Steve Wozenski

Published by Open Books, 1631 Grant Street, Berkeley, California 94703

ISBN: 0-931-416-09-4

Printed in the United States of America.
10 9 8 7 6 5 4 3 2 1

To the memory of Lynnelle,
who believed in me and in this book,
and in the value of the dark.

C O N T E N T S

ACKNOWLEDGEMENTS

This book began as a series of letters to my friend, Lynnelle—a report to her and to Gallery Route One from the field, as it were—while I trudged around Leningrad trying to organize an exchange of exhibitions. Without her and without the support and enthusiasm of Gallery Route One, this project would never have been realized, and my life would never have become so inextricably and so wonderfully woven with those of the unofficial artists.

I have taken some intentional liberties with the sequence of events for the sake of clarity and cohesion. I also take responsibility for any misunderstandings or misrepresentations that may have occurred because of my less than perfect command of Russian.

I am grateful to all the members of Leningrad's Tovarishchestvo, the organization of independent artists, who, whether participants in the Point Reyes show or not, have welcomed me into their homes and their hearts. Alex and Lyuba Kan have fed and sheltered me in times of need, and plied me with wine and introductions, concern and affection; Alyona Bitkolova has trusted and cared for me and become daughter and friend; Valentin Gerasimenko and Elena Figurina have shared everything, in Russia and America, from the most pedestrian of errands to the most hilarious of evenings; Yul Rybakov has advised, informed and protected me; Bob Koshelokhov has challenged me with his wise analyses of the artists' work; Valery Shalabin has translated endless hours under the most exasperating conditions; Zhenya and Galia Orlov have taken me travelling to places I would otherwise never have seen. And lastly, Sergei Kovalskii has been and continues to be my chief colleague. His vision of the possibilities of the art exchange mobilized the artists' network in the first place. Sergei's willingness to draw up lists, make phone calls and plan ahead, and his imperturbability in dealing with a semi-grammatical, opinionated American have made him a working partner without peer. And a good friend.

My special thanks to the Tides Foundation which has seen fit to fund some of my wilder adventures; to my friends in Berkeley who have loved and advised me—especially Susan Griffin, Benina Berger-Gould, Steve Most and Claire Schoen, Claire Greensfelder, Wendy Roberts, Fran and Joanna Macy, Bill Mandel, Arkady and Zhenya Alexeev, Irina Valioulina—and to my family who tenderly indulge my passions.

Finally, to my agent, Ruth Nathan, whose enthusiasm has encouraged me, and to Dorothy Wall who patiently, persistently, helped me to bring order out of the chaos of this manuscript: I could never have done it without her.

Author's Note: Throughout this book I refer to the city of Leningrad, which in 1991 officially reverted to its original name of St. Petersburg, as "Leningrad." Old habits die hard. And it seems less confusing to be consistent.

Nearly a decade ago, very soon after I met her, I learned that Barbara Hazard had another life. It took place through the looking glass we called the *cold war*, halfway around the globe, in the land known then as the Soviet Union. She was one of many citizen diplomats who went without the help of the state department, consulates, or foreign policy advisors, to establish some kind of human connection directly with Soviet citizens. Unofficially and with little central organization, farmers went to meet farmers, doctors to meet doctors, therapists to meet therapists, teachers and artists to meet their counterparts behind enemy lines, in an effort to end the terrible arms race which seemed in those years to threaten life itself. If governments will not do it, these diplomats said, then we will do it ourselves, person to person.

As far as I know nothing quite like this has happened before in history, and if Barbara's story were simply one more example that would be sufficient. But her story is much more. On successive journeys she traveled deeper and deeper into this land, grew more intimate with her friends there, began to speak more and more Russian, began to take on the gestures, humor, caste of mind, even daily habits of this other place, until finally, one could not say clearly whether she was leaving here to visit there or there to visit here.

Those of us fortunate enough to be in her circle of friends here found gradually that we had by association inherited the acquaintance of a whole circle of friends there. At first we simply saw them in the slides Barbara would bring back for us to see. Seated at a table in someone's kitchen would be six or seven men and women, sometimes a child or two. Paintings were on the walls; books stacked, or you might say crowded, into the very small spaces people occupy there; food, growing over the years increasingly difficult to obtain, set out on the table. Barbara would give each face a name and each name a story until bit by bit we felt we were familiar. There was the thin, pale man who had been in the gulag. And here he was still taking risks, an unofficial artist. There were marriages, romances, divorces, parties, competitions, jealousies, summer vacations. All the drama which comes with living. Then, after a while, we began to meet a few of the principals ourselves. Sergei came over once. Elena twice. Irina came to stay. When Barbara would depart again we would send our greetings; we were involved.

And if our meetings were often brief, we had the paintings to give us a swift, sharp glance into these souls. It began with the slides and then the paintings Barbara bought and hung in her home and finally the wonderful show of Leningrad artists, a treasure of images, displayed in a gallery in Northern California, at the edge of the Pacific ocean. The paintings affected us all. One cannot say exactly how. In each case it must be different. I know from watching Barbara's work over the years that her palette changed, took on more red, a deeper orange, heavier contrasts. For myself all I can say is that in a certain region of my mind a series of intense, dense images are engraved, and this is a region of heavy flavors, and yet paradoxically, white nights, and a certain lightness which seems to occupy the architecture of St. Petersburg.

So now it is your turn to make this journey. Open the book. Read. Turn the pages. Become more engrossed. Let yourself make new friends, be moved and amazed by this story, so that now you too will be able to weep with joy not only because we have survived these times, but because *they* have too.

Susan Griffin, Berkeley, 1992

OFF NEVSKY PROSPEKT

LIFE AMONG LENINGRAD'S UNOFFICIAL ARTISTS

BARBARA J. HAZARD

*O*ccasionally one stumbles upon a slice of events, a cross-section of the geology of an era, that allows one to become witness to crucial changes in the lives of others. It so happened that, through a project dreamed up at a rural California art gallery in the fall of 1986, I became involved with a group of Leningrad artists during the first years of Gorbachev's move into power. As we struggled to realize our dream of an art exhibit of their work in California, I was offered a unique glimpse into Russian culture just as the lid began to open.

▲ ▲ ▲

I had first come to Leningrad in 1983 with a delegation from the Association for Humanistic Psychology and had decided to return the following year. It was an impulsive decision. A brief meeting of minds in Tbilisi about the goals of therapy, an invitation to talk further with an art-lover in Moscow, an encounter with a woman in a polka dot blouse who helped me when I was lost—these were the images I carried home to America. But I had a sense that, in the darkness of Russia, I might come to understand something about America and about the meaning of art. I began to study Russian.

During my return trip to Leningrad in 1984, I became aware that there was such a thing as an "unofficial" art scene. Redheaded Alex Kan, then a Leningrad high school teacher and underground jazz impresario, had invited me to a large show of portraits by unofficial artists. It was a September Sunday afternoon. Families were out enjoying the last of the mild weather: young fathers pushing strollers, grandparents holding the hands of well-bundled tots. The leaves underfoot and overhead were golden, the buildings were golden, and the sky a soft gray. We scuffed along from the bus stop kicking leaves and complaining about the end of summer.

The Kirov House of Culture where the show hung is a prewar megastructure designed to resemble a boat, ponderous and barely afloat with meeting rooms, exhibition and concert halls. That Sunday the buffets and the exhibition hall were jammed. Art work hung two or three pieces high, Uffizi style, in a single large room. The paintings were raucous and wild, tender and obsessive, with hints of Kandinsky, of Chagall, of constructivism. Images from icons hung cheek-by-jowl with abstractions or portraits of men in space ships. About a hundred artists exhibited perhaps four hundred works. Handwritten labels gave the name of the artist, year of birth, and title of work.

Some of the artists stood by their work soliciting criticism and praise. "Do you like it? It's something new for me. No, no, that's not at all the point. Don't you remember the one I did last year, mostly red...." Everyone was talking and arguing, gesticulating, pulling each other by the arm to look at something across the room. Clumps of viewers aggregated around particular works, chortling over bits of text or allusions lost on me. Alex tried to explain, "That's John Lennon, see, but in the pose of a famous picture of Lenin," or "That refers to an icon we all know, only it's in modern dress," but it was too crowded and noisy to talk. I came away simply knowing that something was very much alive in Leningrad and that I wanted to see more.

The exhibiting group I saw that day called itself the Tovarish-chestvo, the Fellowship for Experimental Art, also known familiarly as the "TEII"—an unsanctioned union of about a hundred and forty unofficial artists. "Unofficial" did not mean dissident or underground, it simply meant that the artists were not members of the Artists Union.

In the Soviet Union at that time, in order to be recognized as a professional artist one had to belong to the union. This involved graduation from an approved institute of art and certification by a union committee. Membership carried certain privileges and opportunities taken for granted in America: permission to rent studio space, to buy art supplies at union stores, to show work and to sell it. Without these permissions an artist had to work at home or on the sly in basements, attics or condemned buildings and buy paints at general stores where the supply has been short and intermittent. According to Soviet law, unofficial artists could not call themselves professional artists no matter how much time they actually spent at their art nor how good their art might be. Unlike union artists who received commissions from the state and could work full-time on their art, the unofficials were forced, by law, to work at a regular job "for bread" and do their art in their free time.

▲ ▲ ▲

Union artists, although they had time and financial support for their work, were also subject to strict controls. Since the early thirties, Soviet artists had been isolated from contemporary western influences; art education was controlled by the monopolistic Artists Union which promoted the dogma that art should educate people in the spirit of building communism and should be an instrument of state policy. The union constitution clearly stated that socialist realism was the highest attainment in the development of art, and that tendencies towards abstraction, expressionism or images of anything negative were "decadent." In Stalin's day artists had been executed or imprisoned for failure to conform; many of the best fled the country. As recently as 1980 artists were still leaving, unable to work honestly or to show what they had done. "Art in Leningrad lost a lot of blood in the '70s," my colleague Sergei told me later.

Repression and isolation had taken their toll on those who remained, both within and outside the union. The union art exhibits I had seen, usually in arenas formerly used to train the Tsar's elite cavalry, were filled with heroic portraits, war-scenes, noble peasants plowing the spring soil or sending their sons off to war. Most traces of the artists' personalities had been obliterated by years of academic training and supervision by the union. "At a fast gallop would still be the best way to move through such exhibits," a Moscow friend once commented as we staggered out of one such marathon.

Unofficial artists like those whose work I had seen with Alex, who for all the reasons suggested above had chosen not to join the union, and who by and large had no such backlog of rigid training to overcome, suffered multiple wounds. The lack of recognition as professional artists was one of the most painful. "They tell us everything is just fine, we have our 'club' and can show from time to time, but the fact is, we don't have the right to be called artists in our own country," one of them told me.

▲ ▲ ▲

By November 1986, Gorbachev had been in office for a year and a half. Thirty years of Stalin's devastation—millions of citizens forced off the land into starvation or sent to "the camps" to die—had been followed by the loss of twenty millions in World

War II. The brief budding of the arts under Khrushchev had been severely curtailed by twenty years of Breshnev's heavy hand. Dissenting artists were once again sent to prison or psychiatric hospitals, exhibits of non-conformist works bulldozed or raided by the militia. It was hard to believe that anything might change for the better. Yet Gorbachev's proposals for openness in the media ("glasnost") and for restructuring of the country's economy ("perestroika") were beginning to be viewed with a glimmer of optimism by the artists. "What if...?" was the phrase I heard most often.

Small chinks in the repression were beginning to be evident. Letters to the Editor columns in Pravda filled with signed complaints about petty injustices: favoritism in promotions, under-the-table deals, non-delivery of mail. There was a live national call-in program on TV where people spoke about their lives with new honesty. Rumors circulated about publication of hitherto proscribed works by Pasternak, Rybakov, maybe even Solzhenitsyn. Closer to home, my Leningrad poet friend, Arkady Dragomoshchenko, had been promised a visa to lecture in America. Several members of the Artists Union had exhibited with non-union artists without incident. As yet, however, the Artists Union had a stranglehold on the arts, exhibits from foreign countries were only rumors, and the possibility of showing or travelling abroad, especially for non-conformists, was raving fantasy. It was into this milieu that I stepped one dark November day with a proposal for an exchange of art exhibits between our gallery and twenty Leningrad artists.

▲ ▲ ▲

The idea of the exchange arose in an offhand way. I had had little contact with Gallery Route One except through my friend Lynnelle, who had become a member, but everyone in the area knew about the gallery. Located on the coastal highway which runs north from San Francisco through the rural town of Point Reyes Station, the gallery consists of about twenty-five artist members who rent the space, buy the supplies and do all the work themselves. They meet monthly to discuss business, plan future events and talk about their work. Although initially the artists rented the space mainly to show their own work, the gallery had been increasingly reaching out to other artists and ethnic communities, inviting them to show. It was at one of these happenings, a show of art by contemporary Hungarian artists curated by artist-member Ted Odza, that I dropped the suggestion of an exchange with Leningrad artists.

The suggestion struck a chord. Artists are always trying to figure out how they can do something for the world and still do their art. In 1986, with "evil empire" rhetoric issuing from the White House and nuclear weapons multiplying on both sides of the Iron Curtain, an exchange with "the enemy" that might show Russians with a human face was an exciting idea. Gallery Route One drafted an open letter to "our friends in Leningrad" and sent me off to see what I could do.

▲ ▲ ▲

This book is a story on several levels. On one level, it is the story of a collaborative effort to arrange an exhibit of Leningrad art work in Point Reyes Station, California. On another level, it is a glimpse into a pivotal time of social change in the Soviet Union, written day-to-day as I experienced it. We are seeing the repercussions today. It is the story of a group of Soviet artists: Sergei and Alyona, Yul, Elena and Valentin—how they struggled to live creative lives in a repressive system and what has become of them and of the association they formed during these first years of perestroika. And it is my personal journey into a world until recently closed to ordinary Americans, and my search to understand what it was that so drew me to Russia.

▲ ▲ ▲

When I arrived in Leningrad carrying the gallery's invitation, talk had already sprung up in the Soviet Union about "joint ventures" with the West. Everyone was trying to figure out what that meant and how to get involved. But how I was to find and choose twenty interesting artists from Leningrad and how to arrange shipment of the work to the United States were open questions.

Alex and I settled into the corner of a buffet in the basement of a music hall. It was one of those ungraciously functional operations—crumbling black and white tile floor, formica tables, aluminum chairs, someone else's cigarette stubs. Open-faced salami and cheese sandwiches curled drily behind the glass counter.

"Your proposal is a real plum," Alex said. "A chance for twenty artists to show and maybe even to travel to San Francisco.... All Leningrad will become painters to participate." I would have no trouble finding work to look at, Alex thought, but only in keeping the project limited to twenty. Ultimately, however, when we were ready to export the work, we would probably need permission from the Artists Union; the union might well insist that we select "good" artists—namely union artists—who would in their eyes better represent the city of Leningrad. By looking at as much work as possible, both official and unofficial, *before* seeking union permission for the exchange, I would be in a stronger position to insist on the inclusion of the artists I wanted. This would undoubtedly be the unofficial, non-union, Tovarishchestvo artists.

"And as for them," said Alex, "let's start with Sergei Kovalskii. He knows everybody."

PART I

November – December

1986

*S*ergei's apartment, filled with cigarette smoke and steaming tea, was darkly claustrophobic. Every surface was covered with art work, books and magazines, piles of papers, photos, slides, notes, cassettes, teacups, dried flowers, cigarette packs. It was not atypical. Sergei and his wife, Alyona, live on the fourteenth floor of one of those Brezhnev-era concrete buildings that surround all major Soviet cities, in a living room/bedroom with a small kitchen and entry hall. Sergei, not being a member of the Artists Union, has not been granted studio space, so he and Alyona have bisected their room with a ceiling-high bookcase behind which, by the window, he paints. Alyona, although employed as a bookkeeper, is a weaver. Her territory is the kitchen where she stores her yarn and small hand looms.

Sergei put down his mug and stretched his fingers. He is as dark as his paintings. "We have an expression," he said, "'iskusstvennik,' artificialnik. It's a person always working in artificial light. It's abnormal. For seven years I covered the window and worked in artificial light because the daylight wasn't sufficient. My eye had become adapted to artificial light. After a while you can't work in daylight anymore, but the work—it should be able to be seen in any sort of light. How will the colors look when the work finally sees the daylight? All this is no good."

We had been talking, over tea, about the logistics of organizing an exhibition in California of work by Leningrad unofficial artists. Alex had brought me over to Sergei's apartment and, once he saw that I could fend for myself in Russian, pled a previous appointment and left. Inevitably, conversation led to the difficulties of continuing to work creatively under stringent state restrictions, and to concerns about how work produced under such stressful conditions would appear to Western eyes. "You will have to look at the work yourself, Barbara," Sergei said, a bit dubiously, "and we will look at yours. Then we will decide as a group how to proceed. Lots of tourists come here and see our work and promise to organize a show for us, but they leave and we never hear from them again. It has been very disappointing to us. But I myself have recently been having a very strong urge to organize just such an exchange, and the fact that you bring a letter of invitation..., well, that is very good. I will call up the leadership committee and we will meet again on Sunday, okay?"

▲ ▲ ▲

When Sergei and I arrived at the meeting Sunday afternoon, the entry hall was already full of jackets and hats and the sound of men's voices. Our host, Zhenya Orlov greeted us, and I shook hands all around, trying to catch a few names—Yulii, Valentin, Volodya—all men, all in their thirties or forties, all bearded and all, somehow, wearing brown sweaters. Two women came out from the kitchen briefly to greet us. Valery Shalabin, a tall Rasputinish soul with shoulder-length black hair who spoke English, took me in hand, as Sergei plunged into the thick of several heated conversations.

This apartment was less crowded than many I had seen, notwithstanding the piano and the numerous bookcases. Over the piano was a cross; small icon paintings hung over the doorway. I noticed several books about the mystic painter, Nikolai Roerich. The omnipresent beige print wallpaper was almost obscured by bright paintings, a bit kitschy but appealing. It was the work of our host, Zhenya, a soft-spoken man in his 30s with a vibrant light brown beard. His hard-edged geometrically abstracted scenes, many with churches or crosses, were softened by carefully graded flat colors. Some had copper coins attached—that was the kitschy part. Something gentle and wistful about the work touched me. In one canvas, a street scene, a young boy stood by a ripe sunflower gazing enigmatically at the viewer.

We settled in around the table. Valery had translated our gallery's invitation into Russian and read it aloud. The artists asked many questions about the gallery and the artists. Are they famous artists? Why do they choose to live in the country instead of the city? Are they the only artists in the area? The Leningrad group approved of the idea that many of the American artists had moved to Point Reyes to get away from the city, to live among a community of friends. They asked how a member-run organization works in America: who chooses the director? who plans the exhibitions? who decides the prices of work? how much do paintings cost? how does one become a member? While there had been some talk in the Soviet Union about the formation of co-ops, nobody knew much about them.

The room was warm, the radiators chunking away under the windows. By five o'clock it was dark outside. We took turns showing slides: a half-hour for slides of Leningrad artists, a half-hour for Point Reyes. The projector was tiny and ancient: slides fit into a double frame and required constant attention to slip them in and take them out. The teapot circulated. Quick idiomatic comments were flying, jokes I didn't get. "It's not important," Valery would say when I asked. The men tried to guess whether paintings I showed were women's work or not and were unashamedly surprised if something strong was done by a woman. "Well, she really paints like a man," said Valentin admiringly, scratching his beard.

While we looked at slides of the Tovarishchestvo work, Sergei pressed me, "So, do you like it? No? You don't want to see more of his work? Yes, you do? Maybe yes for the show? Okay, we'll go see him."

"Aren't there any women artists?" I complained. Earlier, when Valery had read the Gallery Route One's request that half of the artists in the show be women, the men had laughed: there aren't that many good women artists in Leningrad, they assured me.

"You're never going to get half women for this show, they just don't exist. You should just find out who does good work and not bother about whether it's a man or a woman. That's what we do."

Sergei made a list of the artists whose work I said I liked, and the group added a few others—mostly themselves, I figured—and we made dates for me to meet the artists and see their work in person. Over ratatouille, pickled mushrooms and potatoes, we talked about art in the West: who's popular, what kind of work is "in." The Leningrad artists were as well informed as I, or better, but to date all they knew about contemporary western art came from magazines brought in by such as me. Chances to see the actual work didn't exist in Leningrad. Maybe soon it will change, they said dubiously.

I left feeling strangely excited. Sergei later confessed that he had been afraid the group wouldn't like the Americans' work and so wouldn't want to support the idea of an exchange. "Some of it, face it, Barbara, is not as professional as it could be." I had been apprehensive too, but we seemed to have passed the test, everyone wanted me to see their work and hoped that this exchange could come about. "This idea has already captured me," Sergei said as we walked with the other artists down the windy street towards the metro. "I feel the breath of change on my skin. I know it will be very hard, but the plans are forming in my imagination and I absolutely don't want to back down. We have been too long in the dark here."

2 . A L E G A C Y O F S H A D O W S

I have begun to run around Leningrad, mostly with Sergei, to look at art. He will meet me at a designated metro stop near the exit or on the platform by the first car, or at some other carefully specified place. I must repeat back to him on the phone exact instructions to be sure I understand, then he will spell the name of the stop: "Mama, Ulitsa, Zhenya, Elena... etc." He is usually there before me, leaning glumly against a wall, thinking. He has much to think about, he says.

Actually, he looks pretty dour much of the time. Sergei is not a smiler. His mustache and beard are trimmed so that his face, broad, quite pale and with some lines around the eyes, is edged with a clean black line. He has jet black hair—thick, absolutely straight—with a shock shooting across his forehead that he brushes out of the way with his palm. On the street he wears thick heavy-rimmed glasses, Soviet goods, but puts them in the case when he is reading. Just a couple of inches taller than me, maybe five feet six or seven, Sergei is one of those men who get smaller as they go down: his head and shoulders are large but he has no hips at all. He could have been a bass in a Russian Orthodox choir; his voice is an octave lower than anyone else's and I recognize him immediately when I hear him on the phone.

▲ ▲ ▲

Everyone wants me to see their work and to include them in the Point Reyes show. The unofficial artists need, fundamentally, legitimacy in the eyes of their own culture. Since they haven't been through the straight course to union membership, they think recognition might come indirectly through attention from the West. More than anything, they hope for a catalog of their show at Gallery Route One. This they could show to the Artists Union, the Ministry of Culture, to Westerners, whoever, and perhaps establish themselves sufficiently to be allowed to quit their other jobs and work only as artists. I am moved, and feel a bit of an imposter being treated so importantly. Several of the artists have dropped everything to escort me around.

The day after the meeting at Zhenya Orlov's, Sergei took me to a show in a "House of Academics"—not nearly as impressive as its title, it is really just a neighborhood building in an outlying district where children of the Academy of Sciences personnel learn ballet and practice orchestra. One of the many subgroups of the Tovarishchestvo, the Mitki, had convinced the administration of this culture center to let them hang their work in the ballet practice studio. The Mitki group, named after their leader, Dmitri (Mitya) Shagin, comprises about twenty-six painters of varying degrees of skill, safely this side of abstract expressionism. They are said to have a code of behavior that the artists must agree to, and to do various unconventional things—none of which, unfortunately, I could understand in Russian.

It was dusk and the rain was slicking the long brick walk from the bus stop. Most of the trees have lost their leaves, the benches were deserted, and people hurried past, huddled against the wind. The entry hall of the center had a dank grey towel by the inner door; saturated, it had been kicked to one side. Ballet class was still in session, so Sergei and I waited in the drafty hall peering through the glass at ten-year-olds leaping about in underwear and tutus. Drifts of trumpet and clarinet practice counterpointed the thumping ballet piano.

As the children bolted out the door, we eased in. The ballet teacher looked at us suspiciously but continued her conversation with the pianist. We sidled along the walls talking quietly. "It's just as well not to announce that you're American," Sergei suggested. "If they say anything, I'll talk."

Most of the work consisted of small Fauvist scenes of the city and surrounding countryside. I decided that, if their paintings were any indication, the Mitki's unconventional acts were probably not very outrageous. I noted one or two artists whose work I wanted to pursue. "It's hard to judge on the basis of just a couple of paintings each," I complained to Sergei, "but these are the only artists whose work I really like."

"You can't only look at work you 'like'," said Sergei, shaking his head. "You have to think, 'Is this a serious artist? What is he saying?' But you're right, it's not that strong a show and, in my opinion, the ones you chose are the most interesting."

We slogged back through the park dodging puddles in the dark, and Sergei, who had to work that night, handed me over to Valery at a metro stop. Valery would take me to see Volodya Mikhailov, one of the men from the meeting at Zhenya Orlov's. The ordinarily dim light of the street lamps was further diffused by rain and absorbed by the dark buildings and black cobblestone streets. Valery carried my bag and took firm hold of my arm. I have been touched by the way people walk arm in arm on the streets here; now I realize it may be a matter of self-preservation: streets and sidewalks abound with potholes, sunken utility accesses, clogged drains, badly fitting manhole covers. Holes simply open up in the ground where some essential cap has come off or been pilfered. It is sobering to realize how poor this superpower is compared to America.

Volodya had cleaned up his apartment, two tiny rooms on the ground floor, and hung all his paintings on the walls. Perhaps in my honor, it was not clear. Brownish paintings of cathedrals, thorns, ruins, tortured rocks, primal expressions of pain and fear carefully crafted: a bull sends a message to his constellation, "Life is brief, art long." Another bull is victorious over the matador. Volodya, cherubic, balding, in brown of course, explained to me the meaning of each piece. Valery translated, but it was all very conceptual, much was *not* said, and much that was said went over my head.

In one painting the sun rose or set behind a shattered castle in the desert. "This is a very optimistic piece," Volodya declared.

"Optimistic? How? There's no sign of life in it at all," I protested.

"Look," he answered, "you obviously don't understand the scale. See, even if there were a human being he would be too small to show. The thing is, that out of this destruction can come new life."

There is a lot of that revolutionary philosophy alive among the artists here: only after destruction can a new society be built. But it seems to me that from the waves of destruction already suffered there has been mainly long-term devastation. The other day someone was explaining to me why it was impossible to get things printed decently in the Soviet Union. "We killed off all our geniuses, all the people with skills or initiative, and have had to live for two generations without them. Nobody has known how to do anything and even the tradition of wanting to do things well has been killed off. It is our deepest national tragedy. Fortunately," he continued, "nature is recovering in its own way and we are beginning now to care and to be able to do things well again."

I'm sure he believes this, and I partially agree, but he overlooks the existence of geniuses like Sakharov in the fields of physics, math and space sciences, and Oistrakh, Richter, Shostakovich, Prokofiev, in music, and many others of similar brilliance. The genius is here, and has been here, but, frustrated at every turn by lack of opportunity to flourish, it has in most cases been driven underground. What will emerge if conditions become more nourishing?

Over the mandatory cups of too strong tea Volodya insisted I give him a critique. It was to become a familiar request. Although seeking such an opinion goes against the grain of the Leningrad artists, they can't resist the opportunity, for once, to hear how their work measures up in the eyes of the outside world. I, having suddenly become the eyes of the world, am asked to assess work whose implications I cannot begin to grasp, and am faced with hopes beyond anything I have experienced in my life as an artist in America.

God knows what I said to Volodya in answer to his questions about his work: I remember only asking him why everything was so brown. I knew that I hadn't much liked what I had seen and hoped that not all the work I was to see would be so depressing or so patently political.

▲ ▲ ▲

Soaking wet, Sergei and I arrived very late one evening at the Shevelenkos' apartment. This area on the south side of town had been heavily shelled during the World War II blockade of Leningrad. Now it is a mix of new and old buildings, some tourist hotels and department stores, and large "gastronoms" and "univermags," the barely stocked equivalents of Safeway and Sears. Still, at eight-thirty, buses disgorged throngs of people who rushed into the stores to pick up food for dinner. Each person we asked had a new, inaccurate, idea of how to find the Shevelenko's street; because they have no phone we couldn't call for directions. Drenched, Sergei and I plunged down alleys, up cul-de-sacs, through bushes and over plank walkways looking for their apartment. Rain ran down our noses and under our collars. Sergei had to wipe his glasses every few minutes. Our boots were wet and filthy.

When we at last staggered in, slightly hysterical, Marta and Slava put our wet hats on the radiator, hung our coats in the bathroom, and dosed us with tea. Their five-year-old daughter, in bed with a cold, huddled like a Bedouin in a plaid blanket. Silent, chewing pensively at a green apple, she stared at us.

The art was worth the dousing. Marta's work was tempestuous, paintings in gouache or black ink commenting on women's lives: motherhood, relations with men, frustrations of shopping. "I want to speak about the realities of life, not to illustrate somebody else's interpretation," she said pointedly. "I want to explore it for myself. I really like it that, in life, the same thing may be both funny and tragic. That's where the drama arises. That's what I'm trying to show."

Slava pulled from under the bed a portfolio of ink drawings on the theme of war, drawn in the mysterious darks of Leonard Baskin's or Odile Redon's work: an awkward wary sailor stops for a smoke; an exhausted new recruit emerges from the rocks. He is carrying his gun, shadowed by a black figure whose only detail is the thin white lines of his uniform. In another drawing, a man is drawn into the dark by photographs representing both himself and his father; some blood has been spilled.

"All these are about a man placed in a situation against his will, forcibly placed there. What does he live through and feel in that situation?" Slava paused. "We are all interested in the past and in expressing our own feelings about it. The war is something constantly present in our lives, you know, it crops up in many different places and reminds us everyday of its presence."

Memories of the World War II nine-hundred day blockade of Leningrad hover in the air here. As I walk along the streets I visualize Leningraders hauling, on children's sleds, the wrapped bodies of their parents, their children, to one of the common graves at the Piskarevskii cemetery. It is not difficult on these dark night streets to imagine families, hungry, huddled close in unheated buildings, waiting for the start of the evening shelling. On the buses and the metro, I am aware that anyone my age or older probably lived through that time right here. For me, the war was faraway, exciting, but not threatening. I was ten when

America entered the war; I knit squares for afghans to send to soldiers and bought war savings stamps with my allowance. On Sundays my cousin and I thrilled with horror at war photos in our grandmother's Life Magazine; I fervently sang "Don't Wait Under the Apple Tree" and "Saturday Night is the Loneliest Night of the Week" and searched the mirror for signs of beauty.

I am now trying to understand brown paintings.

Back out in the rain Sergei and I argued. "They are both really good artists," I said, excited. "I want some of Slava's drawings, and then Marta's black and white work—it's very strong."

"You can't do that," he said quickly. "Don't you see, she's doing mostly gouaches these days. To show only black and white would misrepresent her body of work. That wouldn't be right."

"That may be," I answered, pulling my hat down against the rain, "but I've got to balance the show and not just have everything in color."

"But your first responsibility is to the artists, to represent them well."

"Maybe *your* first responsibility is to the artists but I've got to put together a show that people will want to come see. But listen, we can argue about this more when we get down to picking particular pieces."

▲ ▲ ▲

I am beginning to piece together Sergei's life a bit. He had once been a full-time topographer but quit a number of years ago to do his art. Now he holds down two part-time jobs: one, doing some very boring—here he rolls his eyes—recording of weather information, "Just sitting for hours copying figures off some tape like a monkey." His other job is as a furnace tender. That he does only occasionally, but when he's on duty it's a twenty-four hour shift. I had been trying to figure out his schedule so that I could plan a bit ahead, but he said not to waste my time, there's no figuring it out.

Sergei keeps saying he would invite me over but that Alyona has the flu and has gone to her mother's for the duration. So there is nothing to eat, he says plaintively, and the place is a mess. As soon as she feels better and comes home, they'll ask me over.

I took a great picture of him. We had been way out on the edge of town visiting a woman who paints watercolor period pieces. I was appalled by the work, and the interview with the artist was so excruciatingly stilted that I wondered whether Sergei was just rubbing my nose in the supposed shortage of good women artists. Or maybe testing me. On the way back to the bus I asked him, and he started to laugh. I never really got an answer to the question but he has begun to look at me when he talks. On the bus I turned and caught a picture of him in his gray leather jacket and tan knitted cap, dark bristly mustache and beard, gray eyes looking straight at me.

3 . CENSORS AND SCANDALS

I am staying in the Evropaiskaya Hotel right off Nevsky Prospect in the center of town. It is, as the name "European" implies, old-world cozy with lots of carpets, an elegant curving staircase to the mezzanine and a drawing room with plants and pianos. The hotel is small enough that it is possible to make friends with the doormen.

The only routine to my day is early: I bathe in my private bathroom in a deep tub of Leningrad's murky water, breakfast around eight in the tiny mezzanine cafeteria, and come back to my room to write, make phone calls, or putter until I have a date to do something. I have become addicted to doing my laundry. At home handwashables pile up for months but here I am thrilled with virtue and accomplishment at the sight of underwear and T-shirts hanging up to dry. It is something finite I can achieve before I step into the uncertainties of my day.

It doesn't get light until quite late these mornings. At nine o'clock the streets are dark but the sky may be fiery red with early sun; by ten it is usually completely overcast and the buildings across the street turn again to gray. People hurry by on their way to work. Lights come on one by one as the offices fill up. Trucks and Intourist buses slosh up and down the street. Every night it freezes and then the snow and ice melt again during the day.

▲ ▲ ▲

My poet friend, Arkady Dragomoshchenko, took me to meet Timur Novikov, leader of the New Wilds, who lives right in the center of town just off Nevsky Prospekt. As with many of the old buildings in the city, the central courtyard is entered through a rutted one-carriage passage. Three, four, or five entrances on each inner face lead to the apartments above. These buildings are usually five or six stories without elevators and the halls are poorly lit, especially at the entrance. I have started carrying matches to read the inner numbers.

Arkady rapped on a ground-floor window from the courtyard and Timur came to meet us in the hallway. We left coats and boots in the hall by the kitchen, and, finger on his lips, Timur led us through a dark passage to the door of his room. The unpolished parquet floor squeaked, rough and uneven, under our socks. In Timur's room the overhead lights blazed. To the right near the window, a daybed, a table, several chairs, a piano; straight ahead, two high wardrobes walled off a makeshift storage compartment. Paintings of every description were stacked, hung, and propped against the walls.

Timur, in his late twenties, is tall with a punk haircut and something of the Tatar about him. You would draw his face in hard lines—straight high brow, aquiline nose, long jutting chin.

He, like Arkady, is clean shaven. He was wearing black jeans and a red and gray plaid flannel shirt and spoke in a fast somewhat staccato style that was hard for me to follow.

His early work, done in his teens, is beautiful—small oils of houses and landscapes, mostly umbers and white, not depressing but clean and soft and haunting. You could feel the beauty of the cold winter. He has more recently completed a full-length life-size portrait of his friend, Afrika, in earphones and Addidas against a bright pink background, and a number of collages on blanket-like fabrics on which he had glued images and phrases cut from magazines, connected with slashes of acrylic and writing.

Many groupings and sub-groupings of Leningrad artists, formed along aesthetic and friendship lines, are loosely subsumed under the Tovarishchestvo. Some of these subgroups, though unofficial, are tolerated by the Artists Union and allowed to have shows in Moscow and in the West. The New Wilds is one such group. Younger by ten years or more than most of Sergei's cronies, maybe these artists know how to "swim" better than he and the current Tovarishchestvo leadership. There is a certain hand gesture one often sees: palm flat, perpendicular to the ground, the hand swims forward like a fish through a slalom. It means that you know how to get around obstacles smoothly; the gesture is often answer to the question, "How did they manage *that*?" and engenders a mix of contempt and admiration.

The New Wilds, all men, mostly under 30 with no academic training, work somewhat in the style of the contemporary German and Italian neo-expressionists, Keith Haring, Georg Baselitz, Joseph Beuys, Sandro Chia. They are into graffiti and public protest. Timur and the other Wilds, citing Mayakovsky, don't limit themselves to the visual arts. Many of them perform with the rock group, Pop Mechanics, playing conventional or invented instruments, running on and off stage pushing wheelbarrows, turning cartwheels, groaning and chanting. Timur and another artist, Ivan Sotnikov, have invented a sort of homemade synthesizer by hanging old flatirons from a metal table frame. Once set in motion the irons bump into each other and can continue to play for hours.

While Arkady and I drank tea Timur hauled out painting after painting by the New Wild artists—wonderful primitive images of hunters and beasts, lovers and rock bands, murders, suicides, and vacations at the beach. While some of the images remind me of brown Volodya's—I think of the bull sending his message to the stars—unlike Volodya's, these raw cartoon-like creatures satirize themselves. Despite their high key colors, they convey a dark irreverent view of predatory living creatures.

▲ ▲ ▲

I am beginning to feel that many of these artists have gotten carried away by happenings and the excitement and danger of acting up, and have left their talent behind to explore this excitement. Certainly their fans are numerous. Group bonding is strong and, in a time when so much is not allowed, that is important.

I can appreciate the artists' need to protest restrictions on their art, and can see that their situation is really difficult, but I sense a bit of perpetual adolescence in the Tovarishchestvo's art, even among the more mature painters. Some of the artists and poets repeat what they did in their twenties right into their forties and fifties. Perhaps because the state takes over so many parental functions—where you live, what you can work at, where you can travel—one is never really able to grow up. It is impossible to either move away or to become fully independent. Either you give in or you're always fighting.

Alex later concurred. "It's one of the reasons some artists stay away from the Tovarishchestvo: the rebelliousness feeds on itself, those guys reinforce one another, and it becomes harder for them to grow to maturity or to say something positive."

▲ ▲ ▲

With my visit to Timur I have dipped a toe into internecine politics. Timur and the Wilds were involved in a "scandal" with the Tovarishchestvo last May; "scandal" means, I gather, any confrontation or uproar juicy enough to cause community gossip.

At that time the Tovarishchestvo as a whole, protesting artistic censorship, took down its spring show at the Palace of Youth. After the artists had taken their show off the walls and gone home, the Department of Culture representatives declared that, as far as they were concerned, the exhibition was not closed. Anyone who had not been censored, they said, could exhibit. Timur and the Wilds re-entered and filled the hall with their own work. Partly for that reason they have become the darlings of the Department of Culture, and are now in the bad graces of the Tovarishchestvo's leadership.

▲ ▲ ▲

That 1986 spring show had been unusually harshly censored, Sergei, Yul Rybakov, and a quiet gray friend named Sasha told me. Several months before the show, the Tovarishchestvo leadership had written a letter to the Twenty-seventh Communist Party Congress and to Gorbachev himself. In the letter they outlined their five years of contributions to the arts in Leningrad and asked, once more, to be recognized as a legal organization. No response came for many months, but when the spring show went up the city committee found much wrong.

"We always jury and hang our own shows," Sergei explained, "and then the city sends through their committee: representatives of the Artists Union, the Leningrad Department of Culture, the manager of the exhibition hall, you name it. They know nothing about art." He flipped his hand dismissively. "This time they told us to take down fifty pieces by twenty-five of our artists. Out of a total of five hundred works! A tenth of the show! Most of us thought those particular pieces were among the best, that they raised the artistic level of our show higher than usual. But the city committee didn't see it that way, and so—it was a shame— we took down the entire exhibition in protest."

"But, Sergei, what did the committee object to?"

"This will sound pretty ridiculous," he said. I could feel his inner computer scanning how best to explain Soviet censorship to a foreigner. He picked at the threads on his jeans. The knees were practically out again through two series of patches; crotch and back pockets, too, had been carefully doctored. He wasn't wearing his thick glasses that afternoon and his hair was falling in his eyes. "Sergei Sergeev, for example—he had done a portrait of himself and one of his wife, both wearing punk clothing. But it turns out that the administration of the Palace of Youth has been fighting the punk movement, so the manager said he couldn't allow such works in the building.

"Then there was Solomon Rossin. He had a double portrait, the two Tolstoys and Maxim Gorky. One of the men from the Artists Union decided that the classics of Soviet literature cannot be depicted in the sort of expressive technique in which Rossin works. Honestly, I never read any texts describing the canons by which you can or can't depict Tolstoy or Gorky!" Sergei shrugged and spread his hands.

Yul smiled bitingly. "It seems our writers can only be drawn realistically. Other examples: Yulia Lagusker had a piece on the exodus of the Jews from Egypt—just a group of Jews walking in the desert—that the commission saw as religious propaganda. They accused the artist, Vik, too, of doing religious propaganda and, further, of depicting the writer Solzhenitsyn in one of his paintings. Vik had had no such intention. 'It's always interesting to hear what they think you've really come up with,' he said."

Sasha picked up his tea mug and held it in both hands. "All these procedures are simply insulting to the artist," he said. "You do the work not even dreaming how, later, this committee will see in your work only negative images, 'not characteristic of our society.' As Vik said, thanks to them, you discover yourself." He scratched the back of his head. "All talk in the committee is on the level of 'like' or 'dislike.' They act on whim, maybe they have a headache, who knows? If something isn't clear to some guy, he thinks he has the right to say it isn't art. If he sees something a certain way, then that's reason enough to take the piece down. I never once have been asked to explain what I had in mind. It's purely insulting."

"What do you think they are afraid of?" I asked.

"You see, I think they are afraid of the simplest thing," said Sasha. "They are afraid of what they don't understand."

"I agree," said Sergei. "This says something about the cultural level of the people who are supposed to govern our culture."

"If someone is recognized as an artist in the West," Yul said, "then it's awkward for the committee to refuse to show his work, even if it challenges the status quo a bit, but if it's some unknown artist, some Vasia, some Zhenya, hell if they know what to do with it. The painting might be dangerous. They can't be too careful. They 'measure it seven times and cut it once.' They give us a hall as far off Nevsky Prospekt as they can. God forbid something should go wrong and the good Soviet viewer might be distracted from the tasks assigned him by the government." Yul paused a minute and shrugged. "In reality, we don't see our work as very dangerous for our society."

4 . THREE HUNDRED SERGEIS

O n a chill Saturday afternoon, Sergei took me to a four-man show in the workplace of the previous Sunday's host, Zhenya Orlov. It is one of the myriad of undistinguished basement operations lining Leningrad's busy streets, with no identifying sign outside and double windows unwashed for decades. Zhenya works there with a small crew including his brother, Igor, making silk screen posters and announcements for some sort of factory, and in his free time prints, surreptitiously, for the Tovarishchestvo. While the stencilled invitations to this weekend exhibit had stated the dates of the show, there was only a question mark for the address, in case,

I gather, the invitations fell into the wrong hands. All the artists, however, carried in their pockets small carbon-copies of the studio address and had been handing them out separately.

The three-room studio was already crowded and smoky as we pushed into the back room to leave our coats. It is considered unappetizingly rude to keep your coat on indoors: friends take offense, waiters and ushers peremptorily send you back to the coatroom. Beside the pile of coats, Igor Orlov held court over a bottle of vodka. Everybody, mostly male artists and their wives, seemed to know each other and to know who I was, too. I had already met quite a few of them—including two of the exhibiting artists, Zhenya himself and Valentin Gerasimenko—at the Sunday meeting.

For this weekend show the artists had covered both work rooms, walls and shelves, with brown wrapping paper and hung the work on top of it. Valentin was showing very delicate paper collages, maybe serigraphs, layers of textured papers, scraps of type, of leaves. Zhenya Orlov had hung large cartoon-like figures in landscapes, often with church images, in some of my least favorite colors, Easter-egg greens and ducky-yellows with lots of dots. The ones in his apartment seemed much more subtle. Another Zhenya, Zhenya Tykotsky, had a series of etchings called "Their Home is the Road." Chagall-like images of Jewish families. Some messy ink marred the edges. My printmaking teachers would never have stood for the absence of clear whites, but they were haunting and I kept coming back to them.

The fourth artist, Vadim Voinov, made social-commentary collages out of scraps of newspaper, pieces of pipe, hardware, handles. They were based, I was told, on classical pieces. I couldn't understand them at all, not having the context, and they didn't bowl me over artistically, but a small crowd nodded appreciatively as Voinov expansively explained what they might have missed. Everything about Voinov was large.

I asked Valentin how one got access to a press. It is a grave problem for these unofficial artists who have neither studio space nor access to equipment. "I can use the press at my work," Valentin said. "I'm a designer. But Tykotsky has no such access here in Leningrad. The thing is, though, he is still on the books as a member of the Artists Union in Moscow, so even though he quit and joined up with us after his move here, they still let him use state equipment there. Every so often he goes down to Moscow and runs off a bunch of prints."

I wandered into the back room. Igor had opened another bottle. Someone moved some coats off a chair for me and the questions began to fly: who are the favorite artists in America these days? the favorite film directors? what are people reading? do Americans know anything about *Russian* art history? about Malevich? Filonov? Kandinsky? how do expatriate artists do in the US? is their work popular? how much would paintings like these in the show sell for?

Valentin's nineteen-year-old son, Pavel, spoke a little English. He leaned forward till his forehead almost brushed mine. He is rail thin with long hair and touches of acne. "What do you think of Michael Jackson? Is it true he is secretly married to Madonna? Can you get drugs? We have lots coming in from Afghanistan. Have you ever used them? What are the penalties for selling narcotics in America? What issues is the youth movement dealing with now? We are trying to get our government to allow alternative service for conscientious objectors."

I found myself wishing I kept up more with current events and pop culture and could add 150k to my memory. In these intense interview sessions, I feel the hunger to fill in gaps in information about each other. We probe sometimes delicately and sometimes with total artlessness to discover what, of all that we have been fed by our media, we can trust.

▲ ▲ ▲

The morning after the four-man show, a man named Igor called—he had gotten my name from the Leningrad American Consul—to ask me to come see the work of his wife and himself, and to inquire if there was some way they could help with our art exchange. Igor, tall and thin and a bit stooped in black beret and gray coat, met me by the bank across the street from my hotel and took me by metro to their apartment. He and his wife, Tanya, have been waiting nine years for permission to leave the country for "Israel." Like many hopeful emigres, their real destination is America; like many, they long ago lost their jobs and make money however they can, teaching English, baby-sitting, selling their art. They have sold almost everything so as to be ready to go at a moment's notice. Furniture is reduced to a bed, a table and a straight chair.

Igor had little upbeat to say. "'Nothing is more permanent than temporary difficulties,'" he quoted, gesturing ruefully at their empty apartment. "You see our situation. Nothing here in this country is really improving. There is no good art being done now in the Soviet Union," he went on, "and it's a waste of time to look for it. The slick super-popular Ilya Glazunov—lines curl around the block for his shows in Moscow—is the darling of the party; his work is based on exactly the kind of socialist realism the union promotes. Young experimental artists like Timur and the Wilds who try to confront the Soviet art bureaucracy get nowhere. They don't know when they're going too far. They make mistakes.

"The Tovarishchestvo is nothing but three hundred Sergeis painting for each other," Igor went on. "They are hurt by what the West writes about them, critics who don't understand our traditions in Russia. The critics say such things as, 'There's nothing new here,' or, 'It's too small,' or 'This work is derivative,' but they don't understand anything about our traditions: our art is in our lives, not in the products we make, and can't simply be transferred to walls in Berkeley. You'd have to show our whole art history."

I was very depressed by the time I left. I hate being lectured to. Worse, what if Igor was right about there being no good art to be found? Maybe my excitement about the Shevelenkos, about the Wilds and those moving etchings by Tykotskii, was misplaced. I didn't like that thought at all because, I realized, I was already committed, sold on, in love with, the Tovarishchestvo. I didn't want to hear anything against them. I rejected Igor's offer to escort me home. "I remember exactly how we got here," I told him, shaking hands at the outside door, and set off in the direction of the metro.

5. LENIN GAVE US FEMINISM

I have been worried about finding enough good art by Leningrad women to meet Gallery Route One's goal of equal numbers of men and women. To date I have been escorted entirely by men, and the art I have seen has been done almost exclusively by men. And I must admit that, when I chose from the slides that night at Zhenya's, only a few pieces by women appealed to me as having any boldness. Thus it was a great relief to be taken to visit Yulia Ivanova.

Yulia lives a hefty bus ride east of the last metro stop on the Moscow Road, close to the line the Nazis reached in 1941. At that time this area was outside the city itself; now it is filled with new apartment blocks, almost identical but set at varying angles to each other. Yulia just recently moved here from the center of town and now lives in three rooms with her young son, married daughter with husband and baby, a Great Dane named Marcel and a cat, Roosevelt. Yulia, Marcel and Roosevelt occupy her studio-bedroom, the walls lined ten deep with paintings. "It's not as convenient," she said, referring to her new apartment, "but the air is better here and we have a little more space."

Yulia, probably in her early forties, has short, somewhat severely cut dark hair, blue eyes and a direct gaze—an artist gathering material. Her work is strong and alive. Landscapes and still-lifes, a few self-portraits; an earlier series in blacks, grays, whites and reds, simplified forms of household objects and plants, outlined in black; more recent work in tones of brown, gray and pinks. I was reminded of Braque and of the Dutch painter, Nicholas de Stael. On a low table by her easel stood jars of brushes, potted plants and a skull. I had noticed a skull at Volodya's also, and at Zhenya Orlov's. In the corner, a guitar was almost concealed by a purple-leaved vine; some dried fish hung in the window. All these subjects appeared and reappeared in her work.

"Neither the Artists Union nor the Tovarishchestvo seem to think that there are many strong women artists. Is that true?" I asked Yulia. We had finished looking at her work and were sitting at the small table in her room. She had poured Sergei and me some dark coffee and brought out a freshly baked lemon cake. Sergei was poking through the stacks of paintings leaning against the walls pretending not to listen.

"Women artists, men artists! I don't know what to say about it," Yulia began. "I only know that when I'm painting I don't feel like either a man or a woman, I just work. I simply try to be a good artist. It seems to me it's even sort of a luxury to talk about this male/female business. Perhaps it's an artificial question. I'm happy that, for me, it is not a problem. So why don't we just talk about art, about painting, about the artist in general? What difference does it make what sex you are?

"Of course," she continued after a pause, "if you think about it on a larger scale, life isn't easy for women here. Unfortunately our men don't free us from daily service at all. They are for some reason born with this attitude that women need to work to serve them. If a woman likes to do that, if that is her real desire, then okay, let her completely fill herself with that. Fine. But if that's not enough to satisfy her, then men need to share the chores, or even free her totally from them." She rearranged Roosevelt on her lap and gave him a baleful look. "It is because of all this that I had a complete falling out with my children, and with their father. Although he considers himself an artist and ought to understand, still, I had to do all the work at home and totally serve him and my children. How is it possible to be a good artist when you have a full-time job, and have to take care of the kids, clean the apartment, do the laundry and everything else?"

"I don't know what she's complaining about," Sergei said afterwards as we were walking to the bus stop. "All the women artists who have come to the Tovarishchestvo, in whom some spark is evident, have received equal rights with men. When I was on the show committee I *never* looked at the sex of the artist, just at whether the work was strong and professional."

"But, Sergei, the trouble comes long before that and persists long after. It's a matter of nurturing that spark."

"What do you want, Barbara? Do you want to say we are bad to our women? I think maybe this is some problem you have in America that you are trying to pick a fight about here. I don't think it applies to us."

Sergei's response is familiar to me after years of arguments with the men in my life, but I have been perplexed by Soviet women's denials that a problem exists. In the Soviet Union it is, as Yulia said, the mothers who shop, cook, launder, cosset and monitor. State child-care has proven inadequate in both availability and quality: parents must often take their little ones across town to the only creche with an opening and spend many days home from work coping with the illnesses attendant on overcrowded, unsanitary nursery conditions. It is usually the mothers who do this while their husbands read the professional journals necessary to advancement in the field.

When I ask why it should be the woman on whom all these duties fall, the answer from men and women alike is apt to be, because that is her nature. It is "womanly" to be nurturing and to attend to details. The very women who complain about stress refuse to allow their husbands to help in the kitchen. "He'll just leave a mess," they say. And I have been told by brilliant achieving women that what they really want is a "real man," one who will make the decisions and will take care of them. "It is our nature to be weak," they say; men must be strong.

Any mention of feminism raises overt scorn. "Thanks to Lenin we have already had seventy years of feminism," they say sniffing. "We got the chance to be equal to men, all right: we were made to go to work and do all our usual jobs at home, too. What we want is a chance to stay home and be real women for once."

▲ ▲ ▲

I was very shy with Elena Figurina when I finally got to meet her. I had seen and loved her paintings, both at the TEII shows and at Arkady Dragomoshchenko's, and had been after Sergei to arrange a meeting, but Elena was apprehensive about getting involved with some American and had only at length been persuaded by Yul and Valentin that I was okay.

Elena is something of a legend—the only woman on the council of the TEII, she seems to be treated like one of the boys. "She is our heroine," said Sergei wryly. "She paints, plays the guitar, sings like a dream and knows how to fish." In her early thirties, cool, with straight shoulder-length blond hair, wearing a simple black dress, she had everyone hopping: Sergei fixing her phonograph; Yul carrying in paintings from the hall; Valentin pouring the tea. Elena has bedroom eyes and a pout; she calls Sergei, "Kovalskii," in a challenging, semi-flirtatious manner.

Elena has an engineer's degree and is in charge of the heating system at Leningrad University. She lives with her parents and sister, and she sleeps and paints in her small room. The walls are an ugly synthetic brown tile—almost impervious to nails, she says, but not quite. Simple primitive portraits line the room: sad-eyed boys tending resigned cows and horses; a family stunned by the return of a prodigal son; paintings of Elena herself, sad and divided; a man and a woman sitting on a lush green hillside, one above the other, staring ahead, each isolated in thought. The colors are bright—green and yellow fields, cobalt skies, red shoes and shifts.

We had a hard time talking. The phone in the corner rang constantly, mostly, as far as I could gather, about Tovarishchestvo business. Sergei and Yul each placed some calls. Sergei had brought a letter that occasioned much discussion—an application to the Department of Culture requesting permission to have a show next spring. All the council of the Tovarishchestvo, the "soviet," must sign it. Ever since the spring show when the artists walked out, the city authorities have refused permission for new exhibitions. They say no premises are available. "We have to keep trying," the artists say.

There was no hope of anything like a conversation with Elena, but she looked carefully at the small folder of photos of my own paintings I carry. Often when I bring it out, it opens a door: I am no longer a "dealer," but am a fellow artist. "So," Elena said as we left in a troop, "we will probably see each other again. I wish you success on this project. I don't think it will be easy but it would be wonderful if we could really have a show in America."

▲ ▲ ▲

That evening was followed by one of my more uncomfortable meetings. Sergei took me to see a painter named Marina. Very fey and coy, mid-thirties, she was wrapped in a cotton shawl over a long thin dress, wrapped tight as if freezing, and constantly pulling the shawl tighter around her. When I spoke Marina looked bemused, as if she was barely constraining herself from cracking up, and turned to Sergei for translation. This has often become the case—I'm always turning to him to translate from Russian into Russian, often almost ludicrously assuming he speaks my language—but Marina made little effort to speak to me directly. Perhaps she sensed that I wasn't excited about her work. Her answers to my questions were monosyllabic, shrugs directed at Sergei with eyes raised as if to say, "What a stupid question! Who could even begin to answer that?" This did not help my Russian or my interviewing tactics, and I felt as if I was embarrassing Sergei. He kept flying off on side-tracks about records and concerts. If he had left us for a half-an-hour we might have managed—it might also have been hard for Marina to talk earnestly about her work with a semi-articulate "curator" in front of one of the leaders of the Tovarishchestvo.

Marina had been reading Zen. "I can't see reading about this sort of thing," Sergei said later. "Either you do it because you feel it or it's not worth anything. What good does it do to THINK about all that stuff?" What he appreciates in Marina's work is the directness, that she doesn't go back and re-work, re-think, but simply lets it pour out and then stands behind it. It is part of her religious practice.

Marina's work is that sort of impetuous abstract expressionism we have all gone through looking for something true inside us that hasn't been contaminated by technique or art history; that "art" often suffers from lack of concern about form or color or texture. I told Sergei that perhaps I was especially harsh with her; I had been through this myself and came to realize that I really had to learn to draw, to look at things outside myself, to understand enough about color theory to know why some piece of the painting was boring or aggressive or refused to stay put in the background. Anyway, I didn't like Marina's work and felt very much on the spot because I could tell Sergei was excited about it and was pleased with himself to have turned up a woman who painted "from the soul."

I turned her down for the exhibition. "I don't think it's art yet, it's still self-exploration," I told Sergei. "She needs more discipline."

"Ah," he said, "in your country maybe you need more discipline, less spontaneity; in our country we need to get back to the heart, to the soul. That's what we're looking for."

6. CLOSET REBELLIONS: THE UNION ARTISTS ACT UP

*T*he cold everybody was praying for has at last, in mid-December, come to Leningrad: the mercury has plummeted to twenty-three below zero. Ice is building up along the canals and on the edges of the river. Between surges of traffic I can hear the rasp of snow shovels five stories below my hotel window; two matronly women are scraping the frozen sidewalks. Across the Neva River through falling snow I can make out the dome of St. Isaac's Cathedral, Kazansky Sobor, the Admiralty Needle, and that perpetually scaffolded church they are forever restoring, the Church of St. Somebody's Blood. I am back in Leningrad after three weeks in Moscow and have been moved from the Evropaiskaya to the Hotel Leningrad—Intourist puts you where they want you. Although this hotel location is less convenient to public transportation than the Evropaiskaya, it is beautiful here.

At twenty-three below zero even waiting in a metro lobby is torture. The cold seeps into the boots through the floor, the wind rushes through the swinging doors propelled by trains below. While I waited in such a lobby for a friend, the glass in one of the outside doors spontaneously shattered and fell in a thousand pieces.

▲ ▲ ▲

As Sergei and I trudged around Leningrad visiting studios, our plan for the exchange evolved. I will choose twenty artists, sixty-percent from the Tovarishchestvo and forty-percent from the Artists Union. Exhibiting jointly with union artists could help the unofficials legitimize their status as real artists; and a chance to show in America might sufficiently soften up the union, so that they would give us permission to export the work. To have both union and non-union artists in the exchange would be good for our gallery, too, since we would like to show a cross-section of contemporary Leningrad art, not just unofficial work.

Endorsement of such matters can be had only in Moscow, Sergei and Yul had told me, although exactly by whom was not clear. When I went to Moscow late November for a three-week language course, my mission was to find out from whom I might get permission to export the show.

Going the rounds of the various organizations was Kafkaesque. The Artists Union said it wouldn't touch our exchange if non-union artists were involved. I then proposed the exchange to the House of Friendship—they put on cultural shows from various countries and are said to be full of goodwill—but the man I had to talk to was gone for the month. His assistant, very suave in three-piece gray pinstripes, told me that they never put on exhibitions of real paintings, only photos and reproductions. Everyone knows this is not true. We have all seen exhibitions of real paintings at the House of Friendship, but I could not budge him. "Go to the Ministry of Culture," he said, so I went.

"Excellent project," the woman said, "except that our organization only sponsors shows for people already dead." She actually giggled at this. "Well, occasionally, a retrospective for someone exceptional—Ilya Glazunov, for instance. You'll have to go back to the Artists Union." And there, the Director of Propaganda, the public relations man, with a sweet harried smile, told me once again that it was impossible: he was sorry, he said, but the union could not allow their members to show with non-union artists. Perhaps I might find some organization in Leningrad that could sponsor this exchange.

So I have begun the same circuit here as in Moscow on the chance that local branches of the organizations I visited in Moscow might be sufficiently independent to make their own decisions about our exchange. No one with authority is on duty at the House of Friendship—out of town—but I have a date with the Leningrad Artists Union director at four o'clock Friday, my last working day in the country. I will go alone; Sergei says he has given them a piece of his mind too many times.

I am to give the union the list of artists in advance of our meeting. It is definitely too soon to be doing this—I have visited only half of the artists I want to see—but without something specific to react to, the union people won't talk to me. I will have to judge work from slides and hope to modify the list later.

I am now trying to select some union artists. I had hoped to pick some from the Leningrad district Artists Union show in November, but the work was such boring, stereotypical, socialist realism that I could not distinguish even one artist who interested me. Only in the applied arts, theater design, wall hangings, was there any life. So the other night, Alex, Alyona, Sergei and I braved a bitter wind to visit Nikolai Sazhin, an artist who teaches in the same school as Alex.

A member of the Artists Union, Nikolai also shows with the Tovarishchestvo occasionally. He is the first union artist I have visited. He is bearishly bearded with a soft voice and mischievous eyes. Although he has to walk up six flights of stairs like everybody else and has no phone, his studio-apartment is less crowded than those of most unofficials. He paints surrealist fantasies in somewhat neon tones, and does elegant, imaginative, detailed lithographs: bears, lions and mythical creatures stalk the woods. He brought out stacks of prints, exquisitely done.

Unlike the unofficial artists, Nikolai has the right to use the presses in union workshops, to accept commissions, and to sell his work through the union art store. But while the state pays him a stipend for his work and gives him access to materials and printing equipment, it doesn't use most of what he does; his work is just as much for the "desk drawer" as is Sergei's or Yul's, but there's more of it. I almost felt sadder. The Tovarishchestvo members have sacrificed security and money and have to struggle for time and space to work in, but they have the satisfaction and pride of overcoming identifiable obstacles; they lend each other support and are seen as counter-culture heroes. With Nikolai, I just felt a vague sense of "work, work, work," as if he had to keep running. But for what?

Later, Alex said that was what he had hoped I would see: that there is not that much difference between members of the union and non-members. One of the tragedies is how the situation gets polarized. While I was thumbing through his prints, Nikolai lit into Sergei because of an article written by one of the Tovarishchestvo about a recent exhibition where six of the unofficials and Nikolai showed together. The writer had made a case for the nobility and integrity of the unofficials and dumped on the union and, I guess, on Nikolai. "If you want us to mix," said Nikolai shaking his finger at Sergei, "you had better keep your guys from writing stuff like that."

Nikolai arranged for Sergei and me to visit three of his union colleagues. They are all doing original, even radical work in their studios. My overall impression is that the search for their own voice and their frustration about communicating with the public is as deep and as intense as that of the unofficials. Their lives are easier only in that they have the time and the space to do this exploration. And they have access to decent materials.

The work of Nikolai's three friends tended to be more explicitly sexual than any I have seen by the Tovarishchestvo and made me a bit squeamish. Valery Lukka, for instance, showed me a number of pneumatic nudes, sculpted on canvas with great globs of shiny pinks and reds: four nudes at the beach, a reclining nude without a head. Sexual and bloody. The men in his paintings were sparer, with a Giacometti-like quality of transparency. Skeletal. In one painting, an old woman in heavy sweater sits and paints a portrait of a much younger woman in an elegant dress—perhaps herself as a young woman—while a skeleton watches over her left shoulder.

I didn't like Lukka's work at all. "You look as if you think I don't like women," he remarked observantly, "but you're wrong. I do like them. I like them very much."

Lukka himself, spare, with a pink face, red hair and beard—quite resembling the Van Gogh self-portrait he had pinned to his bulletin board—was dressed in tan pants and a paint-spattered black shirt. His studio was orderly, with built-in racks filled with completed work, and a skull on the bookcase.

"What does the Artists Union think of this work you're doing?" I asked him. None of what I had seen fit within my definition of social enlightenment for the state.

"They think I've lost my way," said Lukka, grinning. He scratched the back of his neck. "They figure I'll straighten out pretty soon."

Slava Mikhailov, thirty-fivish, with bangs and ear-length dark hair, also painted in that squeezed-out-of-the-tube shiny style. A much too small rust-colored lifeboat balances uneasily on the black night sea. Grotesque two-dimensional Henry Moore-ish figures lurch about, finger the water, argue. Supermen wrestle each other in a battle of mythological giants. Much agony, death and disfigurement.

On Slava's bulletin board are copies of icons, a photograph of the Shroud of Turin, and a copy of a small watercolor portrait of Joseph Stalin. The portrait is done in soft pastel colors. Stalin stands looking into the radiant future, his white military coat belted low. The horizon line is mid-belly; the artist or photographer must have been on hands and knees to get such an angle.

Felix Volocenkov, who also paints in the highly modeled, glazed style, uses color with the courage of Hans Hofmann and, I think, pulls it off. He had a series of people in buses, tired, crowded, real, and a painting of the Chernobyl disaster. Orange and yellow flames and black smoke pour from the power plant's smoke stack. A high, flat, mud-colored wall confines the disaster, while below, in a cave-like space, two men converse. The outline of a woman, hand to her mouth in dismay, watches from the right.

"I like Volocenkov's work the best," I said to Sergei as we swayed on a rush-hour bus. "He uses more color and the work isn't so gross. He seems to look around him more; the paintings of people on the buses were wonderful. There's more context."

"Not me," said Sergei happily, "I like Mikhailov's work the best. It's laconic. It's got focus. He leaves out the unnecessary. And he makes no attempt to be cheerful. It's good and gray and gloomy."

7 . N O T A D E F I N I T E N O

*L*ate afternoon traffic sounds filled the large square ground-floor office at union headquarters. The carpet was badly worn. Four or five desks ranged around the periphery, and the tea kettle steamed on a low round table. Two men in their sixties were waiting for me. Two women sat at their desks not even pretending to work.

"It's impossible," said Yastrebenetsky, the union administrator, pointing to my list. "I have never heard of any of these unofficial artists, and I can think of much better union artists than these you have named. Anyway, a mixed show isn't a very good idea."

I felt nervous and wished that they had some cookies. I was starving. I have read that you can tell the level of importance accorded to your meeting by the quantity and quality of refreshments offered. Clearly this was a no-frills occasion. Usually I pack a sandwich at breakfast but Tuesday Alyona had been horrified to catch me unwrapping my bread and cheese in their living-room. "What is this?" she chided, engulfed in soup smells and frying sounds. "You don't trust our hospitality! Put that thing down, I'll feed you." Today I trusted too recklessly and wound up with nothing to eat since breakfast but seven tiny cookies wolfed down when I visited the last artist.

I took a gulp of tea. "Well," I said, "I think the work is good, and that it would make an interesting show in America. Of course, I suppose that if we can't mix union and non-union, it might be possible to have two different shows, one after the other, or maybe even one show with union in one room and non-union in the other. The thing is, though... the American press. They are always looking for good guys and bad guys, and the Tovarish-chestvo would certainly become the heroes. It seems better to me to have it mixed; I wouldn't want the situation to become polarized."

"Well, of course we don't want that either." Yastrebenetsky rubbed his neck. "You must understand, though, that if non-union artists were to be represented in this exchange the union would have to review all the work so that there could be a single criterion for all artists. Since this show would in some sense represent the city of Leningrad, we want it to be something we can all be proud of."

He turned to the sculptor, Anikushin, sitting beside him, and handed him the slides I had brought of Gallery Route One work. "Take a look at these, would you please, and give us your expert opinion."

"Well, this is not bad work," averred the expert, fanning himself with the slide pages, "Actually some of it is quite interesting. Yes, it would make a good show, I think."

Yastrebenetsky turned to me. "Then, Barbara, you must write a letter to the union in Moscow asking that we here in Leningrad be given permission to organize this exchange. Come back in the spring. At that time we can make the choices together."

He told me how to phrase the request and said that I should name the artists and ask for money to ship the show to America and to pay for some of the artists to travel. This should be done soon: all budget requests are processed by September—but this is only December!—for the following year.

I got a ride back down Nevsky Prospekt in a chauffeured limousine with a man from the Department of Culture, laughing to myself and wishing the Tovarishchestvo could see me. Sergei was waiting for me at the central metro station, Gostiny Dvor, leaning against the wall under the stained glass. We sat down on the steps while I told him about the meeting.

"That's it?" he said. "That's good. It's alive anyway, they haven't said definitely no. Yeah, that's okay. Come on, let's go tell the guys."

Yul, Valentin, Zhenya and Igor were in the design shop where they had had the four-man show. The place was back to business as usual: tins of silk-screen paint on the work tables, posters tacked on the pea-green walls. Valentin was seated on a scarred black daybed, and an assortment of white camp chairs, swivel chairs and hassocks circled a red and white table. Two old sardine cans served as ashtrays.

Sergei briefed the group on my session at union headquarters. "Not bad," Valentin said, giving me a nod of approval, "who knows, something might come of it." He looked at me more closely. "Aren't you exhausted? Here, sit down, have some tea. You're probably ready to go home to America and get some rest."

"Wait, though, can you, Barbara?" asked Sergei, noticing me edging towards my coat. I was exhausted and starving and wanted to go home. "We want to think about Yastrebenetsky's suggestion that the union jury the exhibit. If we can think it through right now, then you could write a draft proposal tomorrow morning. That way we could go over it tomorrow night before you leave on Sunday." I sat down. The minutes ticked on and the smoke thickened.

Around an hour later they gave me my instructions. I was to draft the letter to the union in Moscow the next day and bring it to my farewell party that night. Sergei went over just how I should phrase this ticklish jurying business so that we would wind up with a joint committee of Tovarishchestvo, union, and me. I should propose Valentin as representative of the Tovarish-chestvo, for, they explained, he has good judgement and hasn't yet offended anyone in the union.

I guess we have all been aware of my time running out here. Although all of them were to come to my farewell party, that meeting was our final working session. I was close to tears on the metro. Sergei pulled me off the train to make our different connections, me to the north, him to the west to go to work, and then we realized that I had been on the right train all along. "Just not ready to part," he said quietly, and we waited together for the next train.

▲ ▲ ▲

The farewell party at Sergei and Alyona's was painful and wonderful. Alyona, hair up in a knot, in earrings and necklace and turquoise knit dress, greeted me at the door. Fully recov-ered from the flu, she had weeks ago returned from her mother's and adopted me. Their two steamy rooms have become my home away from the hotel. I can find it by bus, trolley or train, and am always welcome, and always fed. There are only two chairs in the kitchen, and only room for two, but Alyona pushes aside her yarns and sits on the daybed by the window. She is very beauti-ful, tall and slim, with deep brown eyes and a thick dark braid to her waist. Her father is a Muslim from Alma-Ata in Kazakhstan, just north of Mongolia, and her mother is Ukrainian. Like many women here, Alyona speaks high and very fast. Unlike Sergei, she doesn't yet grasp how simply she must speak if I am to un-derstand, and she often gives up with a laugh, but she gleams with mischief and concern, tucks my scarf inside my coat and won't let me leave the apartment without my hat on.

No one could have convinced me it would be possible to fit so many people in such close quarters. Elena Figurina, Zhenya Orlov, Yul and Valentin came, and tall Valery, and Alex and

Lyuba Kan, and a friend of Alyona's also named Lyuba. Valery, with his long black hair and loud deep voice, towered over us all. All these men are married or engaged but seem to socialize independently.

On this final evening, Alex, Sergei and I huddled on the kitchen daybed while the other guests drifted in to go over my draft of the letter to the Artists Union. "Excellent!" said Sergei a bit surprised. "You understood everything." I am to send the letter to Moscow from California on Gallery Route One stationery.

Sergei and the others have written an enthusiastic response to Gallery Route One's invitation, and Sergei has prepared a numbered list of reminders for me for the next months: whom to write to, how to phrase this or that, people to call about funding. He has also given me a packet about the Tovarishchestvo—group photos, slides of work by painters I haven't yet visited, various typed statements—and a list of records and photo equipment he would like for himself. "But, really, Barbara, only if it's absolutely convenient."

We went over the slides, checking the numbers against the list Sergei had made for me. "What is this number?" I asked him, getting confused as always between the nines and tens and twelves.

"Nine!" he said in English. I stared at him.

"Nine," he repeated, giggling.

"You rat! You evil rat! Do you mean that all the time that I have been embarrassing myself trying to speak your impossible language, you have been able to speak English? I'll never forgive you for that, never!"

He shrugged. "That's it," he said in Russian. "You've heard all of it. That's all I can say. 'Nine.'"

"I don't believe you for a minute," I said. "I bet you have understood everything. Now I don't know what to think about you." He smiled enigmatically and turned back to the lists.

Alyona, who had been pulling numbers of pies from the oven, shooed us into the living-room. This evening the table had been transformed, utterly cleaned off and covered with a blue and white patterned cloth. Carnations stood in a tall vase by the bookcase. Someone had put Miles Davis on the phonograph. Shot-glasses of vodka awaited the first toast. "To the success of our exchange," Yul raised his glass, "and to truly getting to know each other!"

It is painful to leave. The abrupt break is especially hard; one day I'm in Leningrad surrounded by intense and urgent communication in Russian. Everything is funny or important or confusing. The next day I am in America, where nobody speaks Russian, and it is hard to communicate what I have been through. I feel isolated with this secret world inside me known to only a few.

I'm really amazed at how much has happened in these few weeks. I'm going home with two paintings—a gift from Yulia, as yet unwrapped, and one from an old friend, Gennady—with slides from the Tovarishchestvo and nine rolls of film of my own. I have a letter of response to Gallery Route One, and the names of nine artists whom I feel very enthusiastic about. Only three of them are women—Yulia Ivanova, Elena Figurina and Marta Volkova—that's not so good, but it's a beginning. There are still some artists whose work looks good in the slides but whom I didn't have a chance to meet, and there are some women among them.

I have been coming to the Soviet Union for three years, and have had many conversations with people about their lives, but they were random glimpses. Only now, through involvement with this one group of artists, do I begin to understand, to feel, what life here is like. What would I be like had I been born in Leningrad in 1931 instead of in New York? Would I even have survived the Blockade, and if so, with what memories? Would I have grown fat and resentful or could I have kept my creative spirit alive?

I am also having to take a look at the part of me that, as Sergei says, is like the Artists Union. I can't stand depressing art. And there is a lot of it in Leningrad: depressing, disturbing, often raw. I have had to look at it, to take it seriously, to ask what it's about. I am reminded of the question Alex asked the American jazz musician, Paul Winter. "How can you play only such peaceful music when the world is in such a mess? Shouldn't your music express some of that dissonance if it is to truly represent our life?" It's a good question for me to be addressing, too.

▲ ▲ ▲

The farewell party broke up around one-thirty. Sergei and Alyona and all the remaining company walked me across the tracks to get a cab and, after much hugging and kissing and last instructions, I drove away enveloped by the cab's exhaust. It was still stunningly cold, the city was quiet and white. Sergei and Alyona had wanted to come to the train station in the morning to see me off, but I couldn't stand another farewell. This was it.

P A R T   I I

April – 1987

8 . A   B I G   R E D   F L A G

On an early April morning in 1987 our train pulled in to Leningrad. Sergei and Alyona were on the platform, jumping and waving as I stepped out. Knowing how they like to sleep in, their presence at the station was a great tribute. They looked wonderful to me, pale after the long winter, but wonderful. They hustled me off home immediately. "Why go to the hotel before you have to?" insisted Sergei, "They'll save your room." They kept looking at me and laughing. "Why go to your hotel at all? Stay with us!" Alyona kept hugging me.

The apartment was sleepy and warm, the bed still not folded up from the night, evidences of a hasty tea on the table. Winter jackets and hats obtruded into the hall. From the box near the door Alyona retrieved the thick red pad-around-the-house socks I had worn in December. "Here, your socks, put them on, don't get cold." She fixed an omelet with sour cream and herbs and opened a jar of jam made with berries they picked in the country last summer. Sergei sliced the bread. "Sit still, you're the guest, don't do a thing, just eat."

We spent all day in the familiar over-crowded apartment catching up on news, looking at pictures, trying to figure out how to schedule my time here. The telephone was ringing off the wall with people wondering if I had really returned and when we could meet. Some of the calls had also to do with some new scandal for which Sergei is the communications node.

Neither Sergei and Alyona nor the wider group of the TEII had received any of the letters I wrote after I left in December, all sent to Sergei's address. Since my letters to Alex got through fine, we assume Sergei is being monitored. He often unplugs the phone when talking about future plans, in case the phone is bugged.

Back in December as my train crossed the border between the USSR and Finland, Soviet Customs had taken from me my journal, and all the documents and photographs Sergei had given me about the history of the Tovarishchestvo. I had been terribly upset, thinking about the things I had written about the artists that the KGB now knew—the studios in condemned buildings, the use of presses after hours at work, to say nothing of attributed quotes of scathing anti-communist barbs—but Sergei seemed to think I had done no great harm.

"What a pity you had to leave in December so soon," Sergei said, handing me a stack of black and white photographs. "They gave us permission for a show in January and it was a real festival. In spite of the fact that it was freezing, horrible, thirty-five or forty degrees below zero outside! The exhibition hall was one of those huge glass boxes; when they gave us any heat at all, it got up to maybe fifteen degrees above street temperature. We were all inside in our coats, hats, snow boots; our hands wouldn't bend. They allowed us to use the exhibition panels lying around the Ethnographic Museum, beat up and broken. We had to buy canvas to fix the panels with our own money and do it all in this freezing weather in next to no time.

"We put on a show of one hundred and sixty-four artists representing all different types of work—chaotic but a real holiday. We had singing and lectures, discussions, poetry, everything. People came and came. Fifty thousand, even by the city's count.

"The Central Exhibition Hall management decided for some reason that it wouldn't be profitable to hire a ticket-seller so the show turned out to be for free. If you figure fifty thousand viewers at the usual forty kopeks a ticket, you can see how much revenue the city lost. They talk all the time about self-sufficiency, that not a kopek should be lost, but here's an obvious example of lack of business-mindedness.

"We were allowed to use the Tovarishchestvo's name in the poster for the first time ever, and the newspaper articles finally acknowledged our existence and weren't even derogatory about our work. Neither the press nor TV, however, have yet asked the main social question: do we have the right to call ourselves artists and live legally from our art work?"

▲ ▲ ▲

Yul and Valentin came over in the evening and I filled them in on developments in California. Gallery Route One wants to have the Leningrad show in Point Reyes sometime in 1988. We will somehow raise money to put on the show and publish a catalog, but we still need the Artists Union or the Ministry of Culture or someone to endorse the exchange: we need permission to take the work on consignment, financial help with shipping, and assurances that unsold work can be returned to the artists. I had, predictably, gotten no response to the letter I sent to the Artists Union in Moscow—the letter the TEII and I drafted in December. When I had phoned Yastrebenetsky, the Leningrad union man, from Sergei's that morning, he said that Moscow headquarters told him they have no money to support this sort of exchange.

"That means they don't *want* to support it," said Yul, nodding resignedly in Sergei's rocker. "Moscow gives 18,000,000 rubles a year to the Leningrad branch of the union; why can't they spend a little on something worthwhile for a change?"

"This whole thing is a football," Sergei said. "It's just being kicked from one agency to another. Nobody wants to take responsibility for something new, especially if it has to do with unofficial artists."

There was a long silence. Yul and Valentin seemed unusually subdued. Valentin leafed through a stack of Sergei's art magazines and Yul tipped back in the rocker and read a pamphlet. Sergei kept trying, without success, to stir up some discussion, meanwhile perusing copies of letters I had brought with me. I quieted my urge to play hostess and waited, aware that I was getting a cold. My throat felt sorer by the minute.

Valery rang the doorbell. "So, Barbara," he boomed in English, shaking both my hands and bending down to kiss me, "you came back to us again so soon. That's good. That's very good. We didn't know exactly when to expect you. What's been happening?"

"I don't know," I answered. "Things seem to be fine in California but here, it's something of a mess." I told him about the union refusal to help.

"Ah, yes, I'm not surprised. We have an 'anecdote,'" he said. He scratched his beard. "Ivan and his American friend are walking down the street in Moscow when the American stumbles in a pothole and falls down. Ivan helps him up and brushes him off. 'Damn it,' says the American, 'why don't they give you some warning? In *our* country when there is a hole like that in the street they put up little red flag.'

"'What are you complaining about?' asks Ivan. 'When you came into Sheremetyevo Airport they gave you ample notice. Didn't you see, flying over everything, a big red flag?'"

Valery crossed his long legs. "Here, Sergei, give me those letters and I'll read them to you." Bit by bit, encouraged by Valery's geniality, Yul and Valentin began to come alive. It was agreed that I should go on my own to see Marta Petrovna Mudrova, the dragon-lady at the Leningrad Department of Culture who affirms or denies the Tovarishchestvo's requests for shows. Even if we should get permission from the union for their artists to participate, Mudrova will be the one to decide about the TEII. She has limited office hours and even then can not always be found, but she may be the one to help us get the Tovarishchestvo's work over to America.

▲   ▲   ▲

When I called Marta Petrovna's office early the next morning, she told me twice to call back in half an hour; the third time I called there was no answer. I put on my coat and went directly to her office.

Even though the Leningrad Department of Culture is a major city office and is located on the main street, Nevsky Prospekt, the entrance is an inconspicuous door off a courtyard into which official cars hurtle, oblivious of pedestrians. Melting snow from visitors' boots had pooled in the worn marble entry. In the upper hall an affable retiree took my coat and motioned me up another flight of stairs to wait. Alex, who had come over to translate, decided at the last minute that I would be better off without him—he has had some sort of run-in with Mudrova—so I went up to the third floor alone.

I followed a man in a suit into a large reception hall behind heavy carved wood doors. In this enormous room stood two wooden desks, twenty feet from each other, far from the windows overlooking the courtyard. I saw no files, bookcases, nor anything decorative or personal. A shabby strip of carpet stretched diagonally across the room to doors on the far side which led to a wing of smaller offices. Traffic was heavy on this carpet: men in suits and open necked shirts, and women in high heels strode purposefully in and out with briefcases and handfuls of papers.

"May I speak to Marta Petrovna?" I asked the young woman at the larger desk. "I called earlier but couldn't get through."

"Certainly," she said, and she led me back into the hall and through the double doors directly at the head of the stairs.

Marta Petrovna Mudrova's office is huge. Yul's or Sergei's apartment would have fit into it easily. A large thin red carpet covers the floor and a path has been worn in it on the way to her desk. Two heavy wooden desks at the far end of the carpet form an el behind which Mudrova sits barricaded by telephones. There are four phone instruments on the desk; at times she has one receiver to each ear and another lying open in front of her. Mudrova is about my age, in her fifties, with a very blond upswept hairdo. She smooths up her hair whenever her hands aren't occupied with phones.

Marta Petrovna was courteous, and listened carefully to my explanation of our proposed exchange. By now I have described the project in Russian to so many people that it comes rolling not too jerkily off the tongue.

"Very well," she responded. "This is an interesting possibility, but as long as you want to have a show of Tovarishchestvo and union artists together, permission to export the work must come from the union. It is not my department. At the union they know how to handle these international matters. But do not bother talking anymore with Yastrebenetsky: he has been replaced by the sculptor, Anikushin." She looked at her watch. "You may catch him in. You must talk directly to him."

Anikushin is the man who approved the Gallery Route One slides in December. Alex and I raced over to union headquarters but Anikushin had gone off to Moscow.

There is really nothing more to do in Leningrad about the exchange until after I talk to people in Moscow. There I will try to search out Ponomaryov and the visiting Anikushin, and hope, in spite of what Yastrebenetsky had to say, to get Moscow's approval for the Leningrad union to deal with us. I asked Sergei, Yul and Valentin how long they thought we should keep working for a mixed show and at what point we should give up that idea. They agree that this trip to Moscow should be our last attempt; after that, if we cannot get permission for a combined show, we will simply work on an exchange between the TEII and Gallery Route One.

▲ ▲ ▲

My hotel, the Pribaltiskaya, yet a different one from any I have stayed in before, is a gigantic structure overlooking the Baltic Sea, on the far edge of Leningrad. One has no choice in these matters. Visitors to the USSR stay in Intourist hotels; it is forbidden to overnight with Soviet citizens. I have heard that even close relatives, emigree daughters visiting mothers, for instance, must book and pay for hotel rooms. It is partly the USSR's need for hard currency and partly "national security."

I am here this time with a group of AA members, mostly from Texas, who gamely put up with my glasses of wine and erratic schedule. Because it costs less to travel with a group, I try to hook up with people going where I want to go and then to extend my visa. One drawback is that schedules get changed: our stay in Leningrad has now been shortened and we have to leave today for Moscow. I hope to come back in about a week but have no assurances my visa will be extended; I may have come all this way for only three days with my friends, and nothing accomplished.

This morning I woke early, packed for our departure, and watched the moon set over the Baltic Sea. The moon, three quarters full, was a deep harvest orange over a gray sea still shrouded in ice. Finland, Sweden, England and America lay way beyond the horizon. I felt angry and depressed to be so powerless in the face of a bureaucracy that plans my moves for me, makes me stay in hotels on the edge of town, and can decide, with no appeal possible, that it is time for me to leave.

"You still think it's funny," Sergei said the other day when I made some sarcastic crack about being out of control. "When you live with it, it gets to be not such a joke."

9 . THE MOSCOW RUN-AROUND

I have been trudging around Moscow with Yul, who has come here on Tovarishchestvo business, and with Tolya, a Moscow member of the TEII. Tolya speaks English and has been helping with some of the phone calls. Yesterday he called the Communist Party Central Committee for Cultural Affairs, to try to find *who* in this great bureaucratic metropolis could or would deal with this exchange. Leaning into the phone in an underpass somewhere, having after three transfers reached the proper person, he said, a bit ascerbicly, "I have with me this American woman. She is naive enough to think it might be possible to set up some kind of exchange of art."

"That's very well, citizen," the proper person answered. "We all know that Americans are naive, but why are *you* so naive as to be helping her?"

I marvel at it myself. Things are not going well in Moscow; Sergei's image of the football sticks with me.

My first night here I went downtown to the Manezh to look for Michael Mikheev, the Director of Public Relations for the national Artists Union. Michael is practically an old friend from past encounters: it was he who told me in December that the union could not allow their members to show with non-union artists. Saturday night he invited me to an opening at the Manezh, along with several thousand others: it would be an interesting show, he said, and perhaps we would have a minute to talk.

The Manezh is the biggest exhibition hall in Moscow, located by the walls of the Kremlin. This particular exhibition turned out to be a huge show of the work of "young artists," meaning, as Yul once said, those not quite at the door of death. Not a bad show, actually, with a lot of vital work especially in black and white. I was amused to note how often, when I liked something enough to puzzle out the label, the artist was from either the Baltic Republics, from Georgia or Armenia. I've heard there is much more freedom in those areas, within and without the union, and it is evident in the art.

Michael and I found an anteroom with a deep window seat where we could talk. I like Michael. He is in his mid-forties, going bald, with a dark mustache and clean chin. In a movie he would be cast as the affectionate, slightly out-of-it, conservative uncle. This Saturday, however, he minced no words. "You know, Barbara, it won't do you any good to go talking to Ponomaryov about this exchange of exhibitions. He just passed your letter on to me; I'm the one that has to make the decision. It is impossible for us to permit a show of our artists together with non-professionals. I told you that in December. If you want to show work of this Tovarishchestvo, then you will just have to organize a show of non-professionals. That you can do through the Leningrad city agency or something else."

That ends the idea of a mixed show.

I have been getting the usual run-around from the woman at the Ministry of Culture, Irina Mikheeva—the phone either busy or no answer—and have taken to haunting the Ministry building off the Arbat. The guard at the door has become solicitous but it has availed nothing for Mikheeva claims it is not her jurisdiction.

In the end she agreed that, if our Marta Petrovna Mudrova at the Leningrad Department of Culture would forward a formal letter of request to her here in Moscow, she, Mikheeva, would speak to the Fine Arts people at the Ministry and would go to the Fund Kultury about our exchange, but I think she was just trying to get me off her back.

The Fund Kultury to which Mikheeva referred is everyone's hope. Raisa Gorbachev is a director. Realizing that the professional associations—the so-called "creative" unions—have a stranglehold on culture; that all fine arts, movies, records, everything, issues through union gates; that the unions select the artists, pay the commissions, jury the shows, write the reviews, and train the next generation, Gorbachev has said, "Enough!" and formed the Fund Kultury. Its goal is to promote the arts, facilitate sales and exchanges abroad, and to bypass the Artists Union. However, to date the Fund has no funds, and exists in two sparsely furnished rooms. No one knows whether it will become more than just a vanity piece for Raisa.

Yul had come down to Moscow to ask if the Fund might support the Tovarishchestvo demand to be acknowledged as a professional organization. He had a very satisfactory interview, he reported, but was told not to expect anything at all until the end of the year. And perhaps in *two years*, they thought, they could tackle something like our exchange project. Not before.

So we are high and dry as far as getting government sponsorship or any financial help in the USSR for the exchange. I keep thinking about a story Tolya told me about the artist, Ilya Kabakov. Kabakov had received an invitation to show in New York and he went three times each to the Artists Union and to the Ministry of Culture, both of whom claimed it was the other's business. Finally the man at the Ministry of Culture said, "Please,

Ilya, give up. I'm tired. I have not such strong nerves as you and I can't go on like this."

At this point I don't know who is more tired of this art exchange project, me or them.

▲ ▲ ▲

Having seen everyone in Moscow I could think of to see about art exchange matters and to no avail, I went off to two art exhibitions with an old friend, Irina. Both shows were held in what's called "The New Tretyakov Gallery," a building as far as can be imagined from the smaller, more human scale of the original Tretyakov Art Museum, now being remodeled. This new building is a three-story modern Manezh set back from the road so as to take best advantage of the icy wind. Inside, the light is excellent but the spaces vast; here instead of galloping by the artwork on a horse, one needs roller skates or a bike.

Everyone is excited about this show of the work of Zinaida Serebriakova, who painted from 1910-1930, more or less. Part of the excitement is because she is finally being exhibited. Maybe it signifies that other artists long closeted—Filonov, Malevich, Rodchenko, who knows?—will follow. Tolya says there are something like two million works from the avant-garde period of the teens, twenties and thirties waiting in museum basements for permission to be shown. At least they were not all destroyed, like so much else.

I was not wildly enthusiastic about Serebriakova's work although I liked some of the portraits. Irina paced around muttering, "Dead, dead. No soul, no spirit. She can't even draw, look at that neck...," which made it harder to hold on to my appreciation. Standing before the calm gaze of Serebriakova's self portrait or the flawless charm of her child subjects, I could not see what could possibly have made her work sufficiently threatening to the state that she should be relegated to the basement for fifty years. Perhaps this is what disappointed Irina, and many of my Leningrad friends too; that one of the first of the glasnost shows should be so unexciting.

The companion show of contemporary work from the Georgian republic, however, was great—lively, original, complex and mysterious. All the color and vibrancy of life in the gardens, in the mountains, and around the dining tables in the Georgian capitol of Tbilisi, came through. I could almost taste the grapes, the mandarin oranges and pomegranates, the deep garnet wine. Georgians, like Californians, savor the sensual.

▲ ▲ ▲

I am all checked out, my bags tagged and waiting in the luggage room for the taxi to the train to Leningrad. My visa extension came through only this morning as the rest of my group readied to fly home. Now I am sitting in a corner of the lobby of the immense new hotel for foreign tourists, the Cosmos: twenty stories high, curved, with rooms on both sides of what seems like a mile-long corridor. Because of the curve when you walk along the narrow corridor looking for your room, or for a friend, you have no idea how far you have come nor how far you have yet to go.

The lobby is a sea of activity: groups arrive from all parts of the world and clot together arguing and joking while their representatives and Intourist guides haggle with the desk about rooms. Soviets drift into the hotel quite easily; I see a few peremptory challenges by the doormen but most Soviets come through—as indeed did Yul, earlier, for a beer with me in the bar—on the arm of a guest.

Here on the main floor are bars, restaurants, a paltry gift shop for foreign currency, and the various service bureaus. Posters of smiling peasants and boatmen advertise trips down the Volga or to Samarkand, Bukhara, and Lake Baikal. I am also something of a tourist attraction, sitting on a corner sofa typing away on my beloved battery-powered Canon Typestar.

10. ONCE UPON A TIME THERE LIVED...

Yul was waiting for me around the corner from my hotel in Leningrad the day I returned. Pale, blue-eyed, patrician, quiet and totally self-possessed, a bit intimidating, he stood out from the crowd for me since that very first meeting at Zhenya Orlov's. We had seen each other many times since, both in Leningrad and in Moscow, but seldom alone. So when, during our safaris in Moscow, he invited me to come and see his work, I was intrigued. This particular April evening on the steamy bus in his dark nylon jacket and leather Lenin cap, he seemed less formidable.

We crossed over the Neva on the Palace Bridge. The river was still partially iced in, and floes from Lake Ladoga to the north swim darkly by in the black channel below. As we came in view of the Peter and Paul Fortress—St. Petersburg itself is dated from the laying of the cornerstone of this combination fortress, prison and cathedral—Yul leaned across and wiped the window clear. "I served six years in the labor camps because of that place," he said softly. I looked at him in surprise.

"Ten years ago we unofficial artists put on an outdoor show that was knocked down by the KGB. It was a show in honor of one of our favorite artists, Evgeny Rukhin, who had died in a mysterious fire in his studio. We thought it was not altogether accidental. Because we were not allowed to use exhibition halls, we resolved to prop our paintings by the wall of the fortress. We informed the Department of Culture, but they simply called in the militia. That Sunday morning when we tried to leave our homes with our paintings, we were met at the doors by militia and the volunteer 'druzhinniks' and were told we were under house arrest. Some thirty or forty of us got through to the fortress but the militia grabbed everyone at random—anyone who looked like an artist, anyone with a roll of paper under his arm— and by the time I myself turned up in jail, there were all my friends.

"The militia warned us that any more such shows would provoke strong measures, but we couldn't pull back at that point. A hunger strike stirred next to no notice, so we announced that we would put on a 'happening'; 'You will be the show,' we notified the authorities. 'We will not need to bring paintings.'

"It was a very impressive happening. Three times as many militia as before paraded around the castle, even circling the fortress island in motorboats—evidently they thought some of us would swim across the river with paintings in our teeth. The militia were very confused: we didn't have any paintings; they didn't know what to do. We sat around in a circle by the fortress wall.

"Soon a militia car drove up and a lieutenant colonel demanded that we leave immediately. Why? we asked, other people were sitting around. Naturally we didn't get a constructive answer to that question and we refused to leave. The militia told us that either we would walk away ourselves or they would carry us, so we got up, put our hands behind our heads in classic manner, and left. Many people saw this. We were filmed by foreign journalists. On the way out, one of our artists was seized by a passing car and later he was arrested for hooliganism.

"My friend Oleg Volkov and I were very disturbed by these events and, not long afterwards, we stole to the castle at night and wrote in big letters on the wall, 'You crucify freedom but the soul of man knows no bonds.' The letters were five feet high and ninety feet long, visible from across the river."

How appropriate, I thought, that all these actions should take place at the fortress. It is one of those dark granite, golden-spired reminders of the Russian ability to juxtapose might, terror and spirituality—the high hexagonal walls of the fortress, built in 1703 to defend against the Swedes. Within ten years of its creation it was converted into one of the harshest political prisons in Russia. In those cold dungeons Peter the Great was said to have ordered the murder of his own rebellious son; later Tsars incarcerated the leading Decembrists, the writer Dostoevsky, Lenin's brother Alexander Ulyanov, and many others entangled in Russia's dark history. Yet from the courtyard of the fortress rises the Baroque cathedral: its gold spire, topped by a flying angel, the highest point in the city. The cathedral itself a particularly light, majestic, almost joyful testament to the spiritual nature of Russia.

"That wasn't our first such action by any means," Yul went on. "Oleg and I had been writing various notices criticizing the political regime and the social order, writing them at night on the streets of the city, on the buildings, or on trams which then rode around the city carrying our words to every street. We had also organized an underground center and were trying to publish prohibited literature—Sakharov, Solzhenitsyn, speeches we heard on the Russian-speaking BBC, on Svoboda, or the German networks. We needed equipment for this—radios, tape recorders, typewriters, even paper—for recording and printing information. We could not buy it—you needed official permission for that—and, anyway, we were poor as church mice, so we stole everything from Soviet government agencies.

"In September 1976, Oleg Volkov and I were arrested, along with our friends Natasha Lesnechenko and Yulia Voznesenskaia."

"How did the authorities find out?" I asked. We were now off the bus and walking down a wide heavily trafficked boulevard somewhere to the south of city center. It was almost dark and the sky had turned a leaden yellow.

"One of yours, one of ours," answered Yul with a shrug. "It turned out that the ex-poet of Leningrad, Konstantin Kuzminskii, who had emigrated to the US, sent a letter—supposedly to Voznesenskaia—in which he wrote that he was disgusted by the fact that people in her close circle of friends were doing illegal activities, that we would probably all be put in prison because of his letter, and that that would be alright with him; he did not care who read it.

"Of course, he turned out to be right. The letter was read by the mail censor and sent on to the KGB. I saw a copy of it later in the hands of the public prosecutor. In this way Kuzminskii, totally consciously, reported us, and one of our own group here in Leningrad confirmed it.

"Natalia, my future wife, and Yulia were freed three days later for lack of evidence, but Oleg and I were blamed for the notices around the city. Being afraid that if the court found us guilty of political crimes, the remaining artists in the Tovarishchestvo would, by association, be subject to exile and repression, we agreed to say that all our actions had been criminal acts, 'hooliganism,' rather than political; so only the two of us were judged and no blame attached to the other artists. They were left in freedom to live and work and participate in the Tovarishchestvo movement.

"I received a sentence of six years imprisonment in what they call a 'harsher regime,' which I served in Murmansk and Archangelsk, and Oleg got seven years in a 'harsh regime' in the polar regions. He did not survive this punishment.

"For four years I worked at a camp in Murmansk, in a furniture factory—we had some protection from the weather but not much—and for two years in Archangelsk we cut up trees that had been felled. We were forbidden to draw or to write, even to have a pencil. You can imagine what a surprise it was to hear that one of your gallery members teaches art to prisoners. Here, such a thing would never be allowed.

"Hooliganism is a criminal offense, so I was in with criminals rather than with political prisoners. That's a pretty crude level of society, raw and rough, with poor communication and little trust. For me, it was a shock. All my life, understand, I had lived in a tight circle of people of my own intellectual and spiritual level. Then suddenly I dove into such a pot, such a salad, of very different people! It was a big sidetrack. I learned things I never would have learned otherwise about that level of society.

"I had always believed in Russian literature, in that historical memory that says that the Russian people are of high spirituality and wisdom. But when I got to the camps I met farmers, laborers, youths, old people, engineers, high officials, and I became convinced that all these representatives of our country live on such a low plane of spiritual and intellectual literacy that we will need many years to return to the spiritual level we once had.

"You may be saying to yourself, 'Well, of course he met with the criminal world there, not the average person,' but I am convinced that half, if not more, of the people being punished there with me in no way differed from those who were free. The only difference was that in those harsh prison conditions they were driven to reveal themselves more truly.

"I guess at some level I'm glad I went through it—I can say that only because I did make it through, alive and relatively healthy—for I gained an experience of life I would not have had any other way."

Yul and I turned off the main road and threaded our way on footpaths between five-story buildings. The earth was still raw and brown but in the glow of the street lights I could see that the lilac buds had begun to swell, creating a soft cloud around us.

Yul and Natasha, her eight-year-old son and somebody's wheezing father live in three small rooms plus kitchen and bath. Natasha, wide cheekbones, flyaway reddish hair, was on her way out. "Nice to meet you, gotta pick up Volodya, make some tea," she said jamming on her beret.

"I have two sons named Volodya," Yul commented as he hung up my coat. "My own from my first marriage, now at university, and then Natasha's. It gets a little confusing." He put on the tea kettle and ushered me into his studio.

Yul's workspace, perhaps eight by ten feet, contains sofa, easel, desk, paint stand. Papers and books crowd up to the ceiling, a bookshelf has been built over the door. Entering the room is like going through a tunnel.

He pulled a small stack of worn ink drawings from a folder. "These are some drawings I did about my prison experiences," he said. The figures were minute and the barbed wire, high. It was a land on another planet, all geometry, little life. "I drew while I was in prison even though it was prohibited. I managed to save some of my works; some of them were destroyed in the camp, some I could not bring out, but I recreated as many as I could remember. Here among them are notes I made for myself: poetry of the Iranian poet Albayati, called 'To my brother, the poet.'

"Barbara," said Yul, rocking forward and leaning his elbows on his thighs. He often does that: he says my name and leans forward, speaking almost conspiratorially. I could envision him in the camps bending forward like that and whispering, "Ivan, the meeting is at ten behind the chimney. Pass it on." Even if he is only asking me to pass the salt, I feel that my total attention is required. "I never told you, I guess, that I myself was born in a Siberian prison camp? My father had been sent there by the Stalinists for five years; one of his friends reported that he had been reading his poetry aloud. My mother, who had been evacuated to that region to escape the Nazis, worked in the camp; she saved his life by smuggling him food. It was a death camp; every day they drove out a carriage—if it was winter, a sled—full of the bodies of the dead or dying.

"I ask myself all the time why I do all this political work I do, not just with the Tovarishchestvo—which in itself takes enormous amounts of time—but other things: work on human rights, protests against the Afghan war, writing and publishing. Often I feel that my work for society outweighs and interferes with my doing art, but I can't quit. Why, ten years ago, did I do those things that I knew wonderfully well would take me to prison? Why do I continue to do them when things are really getting a bit better here?

"Naturally, the fact that I am one sort of person and not another has to do with the upbringing I had. The conscience, sense of citizenship, honor, love for my people, striving to do something useful for them, not to be just a slave of the system, striving to free each person in our society to be an independent individual—all these thoughts that move me today came from my childhood.

"After my father was released, people who had been in the camps often came by to our home in the country. I heard how many of them thanked my mother for risking her life to save them. Being a small child, I overheard all these conversations between my parents and our guests, I heard what these people had lived through. My parents did not hurry to open my eyes to the brutality of the world in which we lived, but, whether I wanted to or not, I still began to understand it all.

"I remember, too, when I was little, in the evenings—I was five or six, my father just was freed—on the walls of the house where we lived, there was a poster with a picture of Aleksander Sergeevich Pushkin, the poet, walking along a road somewhere. At the bottom of the poster was a quote from one of his poems: 'Someday, my friend, Russia will rouse from her long sleep, And where autocracy lies broken, Our names shall yet be graven deep.' That made an impression on me. Those are the roots of my feelings of citizenship.

"We have an expression: as soon as you really understand the truth, you are forced to act. If I know that some citizen should take action, and if I consider myself a citizen, then that means I have to do it; I have no choice. Did someone have to do something about the prohibition of our exhibitions? It had to be done. That meant that *I* had to participate in it. Did someone have to distribute the prohibited literature? Yes. So? Besides, I knew that far from everybody would dare to do it."

We finished our tea and moved back into the living room. The apartment was steamy from the water we had let boil too long and Yul cracked the window open. The walls were solid with surrealistic paintings of varying sizes: floating islands in the sky, shafts of emerald light through clouds or prisms.

Yul has painted a triptych five feet high and ten feet long that he has never seen fully assembled because there is no room. He pulled the pieces out from behind a cupboard and propped them up around the corners of the livingroom. Mostly in blues, green, yellow and gray, it was a delicate surrealistic piece.

"It's called 'Once Upon a Time There Lived....' That is the way our fairy tales begin. It suggests that something took place at some other time but doesn't exist anymore.

"On the left a soldier is coming back from the Third World War, the last war, running somewhere, trying with his hand to protect his face. On the right, the face of human culture, a classic Grecian face, is being eaten by rust, cracking, being destroyed. Behind it you can see another face, the face of the soul, you might say, of humanity suffering. Why? There in the central part of the triptych, in human hands, is the globe, the civilization we are re-sponsible for—skyscrapers, buildings, more and more buildings. Behind them grows a huge tree, the tree of life, and above all this flies a bird, that spirit of humanity which may be abandoning all of us and may be destroying all of us. You can see that it's im-possible to say whether the hands holding the globe will keep hold of it or will drop it. If they drop it, then someone sometime may say, 'Once upon a time there lived....'"

11. EASTER: RETURN OF THE LIGHT

*E*aster evening the soft orange light sifted through the large slanted skylights of the top floor studio as Elena, Yul, Valentin, Sergei, Zhenya and Igor Orlov, and I gathered. The walls glowed with their paintings: Yul's floating crystal, Sergei's darkly gleaming orbs, Yulia Ivanova's red, black and white violin, Sasha Gurevich's holy family escaping the purge. Tsovik, a member of the union, had invited the artists to hang their work for a week in her studio, to show to the American artist Jamie Wyeth, in town for the "Three Generations of Wyeths" exhibit, and to me. To some extent it was a trial run of our proposed exhibit—tantalizingly exciting. I could begin to imagine how this work would look in the clean light of our California gallery, and how all these deep colors will play off of each other. But how many hurdles we had ahead of us!

The artists had brought meat, fish, vodka and pickles, and I had brought some bottles of wine. Alyona arrived flushed with hurry carrying a basket of pies—mushroom, cabbage and potato—still warm from her oven. Contrary to Orthodox tradition, in which the faithful keep the fast until after the completion of the midnight vigil, we ate to bursting and toasted each other.

Around eleven o'clock we walked and bussed to Vladimirski Cathedral. One of the first cathedrals to be built when the city was founded by Peter, it is one of only six "working" churches in the city. The night was crisp and clear, ice crunched underfoot. The cemetery surrounding the church was covered with snow. People coming from all directions gathered in small quiet knots in the cold waiting for friends to arrive. Several militia stood near the doors idly chatting with each other.

Inside, the cathedral was dimly lit. People stood elbow to elbow. The service was already in progress, the aroma of the swinging censers and the deep hypnotic chanting of the white-robed priests and the answering congregation filled the nave. Because of the large numbers of worshippers it was impossible to see the choir. Perhaps, as is often the case, they were behind one of the elaborate screens to the side. Their voices rose and fell in the close, Byzantine harmony of the Orthodox service, coming from nowhere and from everywhere, wrapping around us like smoke from the incense.

Alyona took me by the hand and wove through the crowd until we were close to the front. The nave was only dimly lit, as if embodying the dark time of the disappearance of the spirit, the days of despair between the death of Jesus and news of the Resurrection. The bishop in long white beard and beehive hat of white and gold and many-colored jewels chanted alone. Around his neck hung a gold bejeweled chain with a cross and a small icon of the Virgin Mary, and a long looped sash embroidered in gold. Deacons in long robes with wide gold sashes over their left shoulders swung censers through paths in the crowd. Shortly before midnight the priest removed the Icon of the entombed Christ from the center of the church and took it through the center-front "royal gates" to the altar table out of view. These golden gates, the ikonostasis, always the most elaborate part of any cathedral, are double doors through the wall of icons that separates the body of the church from the sanctuary. The priests shut the gates firmly and drew the altar curtain.

We had all bought candles at the door. At midnight promptly, the clergy in the altar began to sing softly, and then louder and louder. The lights in the altar are lit and now they sing in full voice, and the royal gates swing open to show that, indeed, Christ's tomb is empty. The choir and the faithful catch up the hymn. A deacon begins to light the worshippers' candles and the flame passes from hand to hand. The priests file out through the congregation into the dark carrying the censer, the cross, the Testament and the icons. Lay attendants follow carrying banners on high gold or wooden poles. Usually the congregation also follows to circle the church three times, symbolizing the women who came to annoint the body of Christ with spices, but because of the crowd pressing at the doors for entry, this could not be. The congregation waits unattended, chanting somberly, expectantly, in the glow of our smoking candles.

The faces of Zhenya and Yul swam into focus, reverent, undefended. They had removed their hats as we entered the church and their wide brows and cheeks, still shining from the cold, were framed by their curly light brown beards. Zhenya's gentle hazel eyes were lowered in contemplation; Yul's features, chronically alert, had softened, the creases gone above his eyes, and I saw again the quiet strength, the ability to face the shadow, that sustains him in activism and prison.

I have been realizing how important spirituality is to these artists I have come to know. They talk about each other's work in terms of "spirit," they speak of "work for the soul." Zhenya follows the path of Nikolai Roerich; Yul writes a testimony to the spirit on the walls of the fortress. Valentin paints the soul of the city; Igor Orlov, biblical saints; Elena, Jacob wrestling with the angel, or the return of the prodigal son. Sergei steeps himself in liturgical music. This may be the radical fringe of the artists' protest movement, yet they are all deeply, unself-consciously moved by their religious traditions. And perhaps generations of belief in the redemptive value of suffering supports them in their perseverance and risk-taking.

Russia is a harsh land whose rulers have exacted heavy tolls, yet the mystical poetry and pageantry of Russian Orthodoxy have strengthened, comforted and provided escape from the harshness. The church, persecuted though it has been by atheistic communism, has served to preserve the continuity of much that is good about Russia. And some that is bad as well: the Russian intelligentsia fought anti-Semitism; Russian priests did not.

Now that the god of Marx has failed, questions of identity are being probed through Russian Orthodoxy: What does it mean to be Russian? Do we still possess the deep spirituality of Tolstoy's and Dostoevsky's heroes? From what culture can we draw images for our creative work? What is our true history and how interwoven is it with Russian Orthodoxy? For many of the saints are heroes of Russian history—Alexander Nevsky, St. Sergius, St. Basil—and most monasteries and cathedrals served as fortresses for defense of their cities. The icons remind us of this history, and the rituals of service plunge one back in time many generations. The old is again becoming revered.

Gorbachev may be likened to Peter the Great in that he is opening up Russia to the West, but, unlike Peter who curbed the power of the church, he is allowing it to breathe again. Some say it is as cynical a tactic as that of Stalin, who during the Nazi invasion temporarily reopened the churches to inspire the citizens to fight hard for "Holy Russia." Be that as it may, the government has begun to return to the Church some of the monasteries and cathedrals which, since Stalin's day, have served as government offices, warehouses for farm products, or even stables. Seminaries are once again accepting trainees. Believers, afraid for years to attend services, baptize their babies in Sunday services. Three years ago an average service consisted almost entirely of women over seventy. This Easter night, although the old women were still in evidence, they were outnumbered by families of all ages, clear-eyed young girls with fuzzy knit caps tied under their chins, teens in punk leather jackets and jeans, bureaucrats with newspapers tucked in the pockets of their tweed coats, henna-rinsed middle-aged women holding the elbows of their aging mothers. Our blue-jeaned group of radical artists in no way stood out from others in the congregation.

I asked Sergei not long ago if so much religious imagery in Tovarishchestvo paintings might be mostly another form of protest against authority. I had also heard that it was becoming faddish to go back to church, to bring out family icons if such still existed. Going to church was anti-Communist, daring and chic. He fixed me with steel gray eyes. "You have seen their work. Not just their new work but work from ten years past. Can this be a fad?" And of course it is not. They are indeed serving something larger than themselves. In the case of Sergei, most of his time is spent serving a more political cause, but seeing him paint with the music flowing over and through him is to watch a religious act.

The priests returned to the congregation from the main entry. The lights blazed. "Christ is risen," sang the bishop, just as the angel who removed the rock from Christ's tomb had cried out. "Christ is risen from the dead, trampling down Death by Death, and upon those in the tombs bestowing life." Censers swung to the four directions, and the congregation joyfully returned, "Indeed He is risen." The bells rang out from the tower above. Everyone turned to their neighbors, "Christ is risen," "Indeed He is risen," hugging and kissing each other.

When we emerged again into the crisp air, faces flushed and half dizzy from the close smoky fumes, the bells were still pealing above us and from across the river and far to our left the music of church bells rang out from towers all over the city like a thousand birds calling to each other in the forest.

1 2 . R U M B L I N G S

I have a feeling that Sergei's increasingly heroic efforts to hold together such an unwieldy group as the present Tovarishchestvo, now 150 members, may be doomed. Internal rifts are becoming evident to me—"nothing new," says Sergei morosely. While the Tovarishchestvo's political incorruptibility is admirable—you can see that it permeates their art—with all the changes going on in the country, the time for the clenched fist could be over. This issue has been on my mind because of the "scandal" that has been brewing since before I arrived. The Dom Kino (the House of Cinema) cancelled a promised Tovarishchestvo show because the association of movie house directors considered the work too radical. Protesting this cancellation, thirty of the seventy artists who were to have exhibited gathered at the Dom Kino, carried all the work from the theater to the street and, propping it against trees and fence posts, arranged a street show.

The day was cold and overcast but neither raining nor windy. The street was a quiet one but bit by bit a crowd gathered— school children, shoppers, people on their way to the metro. "Why are you doing this?" they asked. The militia, properly notified, gazed uninterestedly from across the street. A photographer from the Leningrad TV station shot some footage.

Everyone has been apprehensive about such a demonstration. Sergei has been trying to get the TEII council to agree on a course of action—the history of punitive sanctions against the artists is on all our minds—and then he was responsible for notifying everyone to show up. He has been snapping at Alyona and snarling over the phone. He had told me to stand apart lest I get hauled off to jail with the rest of them. This fueled my fears of violence, and selfishly, I worried that the TEII's combativeness might prove harmful to our exchange of exhibitions.

At first I tried to stay out of sight of the TV camera, as Sergei had suggested, but everything seemed so benign, and so many of my acquaintances were there, that I gave up hiding and shot some film myself. If the KGB is really interested in me they probably already know where I am and, if not, they most likely won't spot me on TV.

Promptly at one o'clock an ancient flatbed truck rolled up and the artists bundled up their paintings. Whatever they couldn't carry home immediately they heaved into the back of the truck. I cringed to see so much work hastily crammed together with no padding or protection, knowing how gingerly we transport artwork in the West, but exigencies of time and of money for the truck rental demanded that they haul everything off quickly for later reclaim. The truck trundled away, Valery and Zhenya Orlov sitting in the back bracing the work, and the artists rushed or dawdled back to their jobs.

Did the demonstration accomplish anything besides uphold-
ing principles? Standing on principle is not to be minimized, but
beyond that it seems to have been a protest without consequences. Perhaps most protests are. In this case, a few passersby
heard the story of an art show cancelled because of censorship;
Leningrad TV gathered some footage for a show that neither
Sergei nor Yul believe will ever be broadcast; and the city authorities demonstrated that, indeed, something has changed. A
demonstration that two years ago would have brought serious
penalties attracted little notice. No one interfered, threatened,
provoked or arrested.

▲ ▲ ▲

I have heard rumblings to the effect that the TEII has become
more of a civic organization, working for social-political change,
than one promoting art. The New Wilds, who now call themselves the New Artists, are among those leveling these criticisms.
I was interested to note then that none of the New Artists, nor
members of other sub-groups like The Island or the Group of
Fourteen participated in the demonstration; the participants consisted of the current Tovarishchestvo leadership and their close
friends.

A week after Easter I went off to see Timur, having finally
caught up with him at an exhibition at the Youth Palace. He and
many of the New Artists have just returned from Riga where they
participated in a show with Gennady Zubkov, Gleb Bogomolov,
and others from the Group of Fourteen. Some of the TEII call
them "The Groupa Dollar": they sell too well to Westerners for
everyone to be pleased.

I had last seen Timur in Moscow in December, when he invited
me to attend two events sponsored by the Artists Union. In an effort
to open up to new things, the union had committed itself to two
weeks of one-night stands by artists, some union, some not, doing
new-wave work. Each artist was allowed to mount his or her show
in a small room behind the large union exhibition space and to open
to the public, one night only, from seven till nine.

The first night, Tuesday, Timur met me on the pavement out-side and ushered me through the double checkpoints—the guard at the front door who checks your ticket before letting you into the lobby, and the second guard who takes the ticket at the door to the exhibition space. The walls in the back gallery had been covered, floor to ceiling, by abstract painted drawings on the So-viet equivalent of mylar—wild energetic brushstrokes in reds, yellows and blacks—drips, splashes, twists and turns. It was like being in a fantasy basement, totally surrounded by drawings. A mime performed to rock music. The artist Sergei Shutov, more resembling a physics professor than an artist in round metal-rimmed glasses and a close haircut, gave a short speech and horsed around with the mime. Video cameras whirred and flash-bulbs crackled.

Two evenings later the New Wilds exhibited. This time Timur forgot to come outside for me, and no amount of cajoling would get me past the doorguard without a ticket. I was not the only one swearing that I was best friends with one of the artists; the crowd had tripled since Tuesday and was spilling onto the street. People banged on the picture window with their palms trying to get the attention of acquaintances inside, and attempted to shoul-der in whenever the guard was distracted. Two uniformed mili-tia stood on the corner and a police car waited across the street.

I sent word to Timur through Tuesday's artist, Shutov, and soon was admitted. The back room was jammed. Two added par-titions created tiny anterooms. Several of the Leningrad artists I had met before were there, including Afrika, gorgeously blond, in a pre-revolutionary military jacket with epaulettes dripping gold braid and a chestful of homemade crosses. Timur wore a suit jacket over the familiar red and gray plaid shirt. He was ex-hibiting three of his new fabric pieces which I liked much better on second look.

The other six or seven artists had brought wild rough pieces in high key colors about violent events. A brown shark was dis-emboweling a screaming underwater swimmer as a green-clad deep-sea diver eviscerated the shark. Blood colored the bright blue sea. In another piece, a yellow duck took off like a rocket from between a man's legs. The lush yellows, reds and blues turned what might have been a parody into a stunning piece. One of the artists, Oleg Kotel'nikov, had hung a portrait of Sergei, dark and bespectacled, standing before a stack of paintings hand aloft in a dictatorial salute, four fingers outstretched and thumb crooked across the palm.

Rock music reverberated. Men with microphones attached themselves to the artists. It was impossible to hear over the din; in order to talk we would step back into the front showroom which displayed sculpture by union artists: quiet, carpeted, each piece separate from the next, orderly, black and gray and white. The following evening the one-night series was cancelled. "Too disorderly," people were told. "The crowds grew too large and were interfering with traffic." I myself never saw more than ten cars pass, but indeed the crowd and the clamor for entry was urgent and growing as word of the shows spread. Perhaps the Artists Union became frightened by the demand they had unleashed. They must be feeling a bit self-protective these days anyway, for they are receiving all manner of unprecedented requests to organize exhibits, both from grassroots groups within the USSR such as the Tovarishchestvo and from foreigners on every level of the art world, Gallery Route One included. Isolated as they have been, geographically and dogmatically, they have no background for discriminating between the meaningful and the flashy. They are afraid to open doors too quickly.

▲ ▲ ▲

This April morning, Timur's room at his grandmother's showed signs of a late night party. Bringing over the kettle of boiling water for our tea, he poured some directly on the table and began to scrub last night's wine off the surface with a wad of fabric, working carefully around the leftover wine glasses. One of the glasses knocked over and he scrubbed some more with the spilled wine, pushing back the clutter. Putting the tea kettle on the floor, he brought over some cups and poured our tea.

In a forum at the Youth Palace the night before, Timur had stated that the goal of the Wilds was to be admitted as full members of the union. Sergei had seemed surprised and bemused; *his* goal is recognition of the TEII as an autonomous section of professional artists, granting members the right to work as artists without having to join the Artists Union. "What about this?" I asked Timur. "Do you really want to join the union? Do you think you could keep doing your own work without interference?"

"I think we would be alright even if we joined," he answered. "We are doing okay without all these political battles. We have a strong group, we're having shows here and there. I'm off tonight to Moscow for an exhibition, and there seem to be some international shows in the offing. I see us as the 'guerrillas' of the art movement: we sweep down out of the hills, shoot, yell, and ride back into the hills again."

"If we went over to the union I think we would die immediately," Sergei had told me. "We have to stay free to change things, no matter how difficult that may be, even if we have to continue working as furnace stokers or night guards. At least in order to feed myself I'm not obliged to paint the sort of crap they would be willing to pay me for. Art under someone else's rules degrades the artist, that's my stance, and I will quite consciously lead such a difficult life in order to keep my freedom.

"Now more than ever we need to prove what we can bring to our society. Maybe we unofficial artists are really the strongest patriots, after all, because we are called on to create values, sincere values, within our own country. I know that sounds like bragging, but maybe it's true."

▲ ▲ ▲

I have spotted some special tension around the forthcoming May exhibition. On Easter evening after the church service I went back to Sergei and Alyona's with Yul and Valentin, and they began to argue about this show. I gave up and went off to sleep on the kitchen divan—my first night's truancy from the hotel—but Alyona told me the next morning that the others stayed until after five o'clock arguing and rearguing: who should be in the exhibit, how it should be juried. The next morning Sergei, looking bleakly hung-over, said he couldn't remember a thing they decided, and that they would have to discuss it all over again.

When Valentin invited me over for dinner later in the week, I took advantage of his wife Tanya's good English to ask for an explanation of all this debate.

"We think that this is a critical moment for the Tovarishchestvo to try once again to become legitimized," Valentin said soberly. "We are thinking of having a show of fifteen or twenty of the most consistently accomplished and innovative artists—showing only their work—and focusing on the major directions of experimental art in the Soviet Union today. The union can't touch the sort of work we do and we think we could attract a lot of attention. The problem is, it would mean an abrupt break in the Tovarishchestvo policy of inclusiveness: there will be screams of favoritism and many won't understand."

I can imagine the uproar. Sergei is already plagued by phone calls about the show: when is it? where do I bring my work? how may pieces can I enter? The TEII council can not yet agree how, or whether, to present this decision, who should be the jury, and how to handle the expected bruised feelings. Sergei stalls the artists on the phone, waiting for clarity from the committee.

I understand what they are hoping for: they would like this spring show to be as important as were some of the avant-garde exhibits in Moscow and in Paris early this century. These exhibits were truly turning points in the history of art. Yet if the TEII exhibition committee selects out "the best" of its members for special attention, it may also mean the end of the Tovarishchestvo as it has been. If their members are not well represented, splinter groups such as the New Artists, the Mitki, the Fourteen, the Island, may simply say the hell with it; and all the individual artists struggling for some sort of recognition will cry breach-of-faith at the elitism involved in this sort of jurying.

"Who would make the selection?" I asked Sergei the next day. "Will you get someone in from the outside the way we do?"

"There is nobody outside the Tovarishchestvo that the artists would trust. It will have to be us." Sergei paused. "Of course, no one wants to do it. It's a thankless job and, besides, if you are on the jury panel you are ruled out as a participant."

▲ ▲ ▲

Back in America I have been in touch with an emigree from Leningrad, Tanya, a childhood friend of Sergei's. She had called me just before I left for the Soviet Union to relay some questions to Sergei.

Ask Sergei, Tanya instructed me, if he still needs to be doing all this confrontation or if he is just hanging on to some youthful idea that has lost its validity? We grew up stubborn, she told me, and we loved that time when we were young, when we were stubborn, but it is over, we have lost it. Unofficial art is not illegal anymore. Do the artists still have to defend the movement as a very special thing?

"Those are very strange questions Tanya sent me," Sergei said. He and Alyona and I were sitting in the kitchen one morning. We had finished breakfast and were still drinking tea. Sergei had just put on a record of Russian liturgical music. Alyona was holding strands of colored yarn next to each other trying out combinations for a belt she wanted to start. "I understand how far away Tanya is. She only has the past to go on and can play out any sort of fantasy about us. Probably in the midst of her hard life in America she reads the paper and thinks everything in Russia is fine now.

"But out here in middle Siberia," he laughed shortly, "nothing, really nothing, as far as the practicalities of our lives are concerned, has changed. I can't say nothing is happening, but there is more talk than action. I guess that's the essence of historical development: step by step you hold, hold, hold, and then, boom, a tiny step, a bit of progress. This current step falls during the time of Gorbachev's rule; if it was not he, in a year or two, another would come along. The time is ripe, as they say."

Sergei thinks what is needed is a perestroika of the personality itself: nothing is really changing because no one knows how to behave without orders from above. Bureaucrats interpret new rules in the same old way.

"Tanya's questions really amaze me, especially about whether she or I could change from what we were in our youth. I think we are truly, deeply stubborn and are not likely to change. Sure, I get tired and my art suffers. I have a lot of plans of my own that I have no time to carry out. But I think we can create a climate here in Leningrad for people to see what is really going on, and we can give the younger generation of artists a chance to realize their potential, to work out in the open in a way we never could—to think things we couldn't think. In our time, we had to make do with apartment shows, to work underground—our consciousness was closed as well. Our big goal now is just what it has always been, to open things up.

"We have to retain our freedom of action and not get co-opted by the union. Unofficial art will always be unofficial; I don't know where she got the idea it is now legal. Yes, they allow us to show, and even to sell occasionally, and we were able to use our name, TEII, for the first time at the Gavan Exhibition, but they make us fight for each new show through all the same hassles as before, to the very edge of a scandal, and we still do not have the right to call ourselves artists and to work full-time in our profession.

"All this will really get on Tanya's nerves," Sergei said. He got up and stretched and scratched his head. The record was over and the apartment quiet and stuffy. "The next phrase out of my mouth is bound to be, 'If nobody will do it, then who but me should do it?.' I don't even bother to ask myself that question anymore." He shrugged and went off to change the record.

13. EVERYTHING WILL BE FINE

Marta Petrovna Mudrova has been thrown by my news that Anikushin of the Artists Union, whom I had finally reached by phone in his studio, unequivocally refused to sanction a mixed show. That decision leaves her with the task of arranging to have the Tovarishchestvo's art shipped out of the country and she does not know how to do that. She would try to find out, she told me on Tuesday, and would let me know Friday. Arkady, who arrived in time to translate the last two minutes of our meeting, thinks she seriously wants to help, but Mudrova told Yul, who saw her right after I did, that I had undoubtedly misunderstood Anikushin and that the mixed show would be fine with the union. She much prefers that idea to taking a project into uncharted waters.

After a frustrating round of no-answer/line-busy Friday morning, I went again to see her. It was truly a horrible day, raining and cold and windy. All week the temperature has been hanging around freezing with moments of sun but mostly gray. Last night it started to rain. The streets of Leningrad are very dirty: the sand they spread on the winter ice is being uncovered by the melting snow and even though street sweepers and metro sweepers work around the clock, there is a seemingly infinite quantity of dirt on steps, on sidewalks, in lobbies, in the trams. Yesterday the tram windows steamed up so badly that dirty water was dripping off the sill onto the sleeve of the woman in front of me.

Everybody is complaining about such an unusually cold spring after a record-setting brutal winter. By this time in April, someone told me, it's usually possible to shift to wearing jackets, not coats. In Moscow, buds had begun to thicken the parks with pink spring haze, but here in Leningrad there is still no grass and the earth and the trees are dark. Maybe this rain will clean things up a bit and encourage some growth.

I arrived at the Department of Culture building dripping and cross. Mudrova was in a meeting but her assistant said maybe she could see me later. I sat down on the red sofa in the hallway at the head of the stairs and pulled out my knitting. Mudrova passed by several times in urgent conversation with others but barely acknowledged me. This exchange is surely a thorn in her side. Others strode down the corridor in and out of the far wing. After a while Yul appeared on some business of his own and sat with me. The assistant, taking pity on us, brought us tea and cookies.

Finally Mudrova was alone in her office. "Knock," Yul said. "Knock and just go in. I'll come with you." In the United States you wait to be summoned; here, if you imagine someone is free you give a token knock and walk in. If they don't want to see you they shriek at you to leave.

Mudrova had indeed talked to Anikushin herself and was aware that the answer once and for all was no. "There is no precedent at all for a show of unofficial art," she said. She leaned forward and peered at me. "I do not know how to begin to organize it. Anyway, who *are* you? I don't know who you are. Whom do you represent? What kind of a gallery is this Gallery Route One? I have no relationship with you, you know, none at all! I have a relationship with the Tovarishchestvo," she gestured at Yul, "and I will work on this project through them. They can let you know what will be the next step." She returned to her phones.

I must have looked discouraged. "Everything will be fine," she said, covering the receiver with her hand. "Don't worry." But I do not feel optimistic. Without some sort of guarantee that we will be allowed to get the work to America, I don't know how we are to raise money at home or find other galleries to take the show.

But I have the bit in my teeth and am determined to pull off this show. The Tovarishchestvo council had suggested last December that, if we couldn't get state support to ship the work, we might find some rich patron to buy everything. At the time I was appalled, but I have now taken a first step myself: I have finished arrangements to buy a painting by Elena Figurina and one by Valentin Gerasimenko. If we never get further than that, I will have those paintings myself; if we do pull off the show, so much the better.

Buying just those two pieces was a complicated business. One needs a permit to take any art out of the country and varying amounts of duty payments are expected, in this case 100%. Zhenya Orlov accompanied me to an office on Yakubovich Street near the Leningrad Manezh and St. Isaac's Cathedral. The office is a small basement suite through an unmarked ice encrusted archway, the unprepossessing door marked only by a paper: "Export Evaluation Department of the Ministry of Culture." The waiting room was already crowded with other petitioners, mostly future emigres getting family treasures evaluated for the export tax. We had brought hastily done black and white photographs of each painting in the prescribed size with dates, titles, and artists' information on the back of each photograph.

Two officials received us at last in the inner room, examined my passport and wrote down the number of the train I was to leave on for Helsinki. "Everything looks fine," they said, "but you must go to the controller's office at the Hermitage Museum and get a permit—five rubles. Come back Thursday."

Zhenya went off to work and I set off alone for the Hermitage. The wind off the river was strong and cool as I walked along the embankment past St. Isaacs and into the long shadow of the Winter Palace, now the Hermitage Museum. It was a sparkling day for a change although clouds lowered over the western horizon. Most of the roofs are now clear of snow, the drains by and large unclogged, and the sidewalks almost free of ice.

The entrance I needed was on the far end of the palace. A receptionist pointed me to a window, at which I was directed to another window. It took a total of seven transactions to pay my five rubles, not including the four times I returned to the receptionist for help. She eventually simply quit her post and accompanied me through the process—her first time also—after which she helped me into my coat, tucked in my scarf, made me put on my hat, and ushered me to the lobby door, receipt safely in hand.

I returned Thursday to the Yakubovich office with Elena and Valentin who had brought the paintings, and with Sergei who had come to see how this process worked. We were sent outside while the examiners checked the work. "They are probably scraping through the paint to be sure you're not really smuggling out icons," said Valentin. He and Sergei lit up cigarettes. We stood in the dank courtyard and checked our watches.

"You will pay the fees on the train at the Finnish border," the senior assessor told us when we returned. "We have attached stamps to the backs of the paintings and everything should be fine."

Because of the 100% duty, the paintings cost extra money that I would rather have go to the artists, but I love both pieces and am thrilled to be taking them home with me. Elena's "Return of the Prodigal Son" has stayed in my mind since I first saw it last November: somber despite its reds, yellows and greens, the returning son dives into the grass in self-abasement while his be-wildered family stand in a row wondering how to react. The good brother does not look pleased. Actually, nobody looks pleased.

Valentin's painting is a small icon-like piece of such beauty and soul that it was the one above all others that I wanted to keep for myself. It is a glimpse of two cities. On the left are paths through the old city. Soft yellows and peaches color the walls, in the background the domed bell-tower of a blue cathedral pen-etrates the gray sky. The moon tries to break through. The sky has been obliterated on the right and the painting is divided by a characterless concrete apartment house. It opens to show its in-terior—an elevator shaft, peeling paint, graffiti—yet the colors are intensely beautiful Chinese reds and oranges, pearled grays and deep sea blues. Valentin has named it "The Landscape That Gives Hope."

"It is a nostalgic painting," Valentin had told me. "Maybe, as the poet Vosnesensky says, 'nostalgic for the reality of the present.' I was born, raised, and lived until almost a respected age here in old Petersburg." Valentin massaged his chin through his beard. Strands of gray are beginning to show. "Petersburg has a special psychology, you know—everyone who lives here has their own city—there is the Petersburg of Dostoevsky, of Blok, of Pushkin....

"After the war, before my very eyes, the city raised itself up again. I saw the demolished buildings repaired, but before my eyes, too, the city was being destroyed. People began to tear down the old buildings to adjust to new needs. Maybe there was no evil in this, but to us, the contemporaries of this city, we felt great sorrow for it.

"At that time, I myself moved from the old city to the new. The new city, as you know, is a faceless monster where you can-not really exist, you can only sleep, rest, and then you have to get out of it. It has no spiritual content.

"In the painting, I tried to combine these concepts—one culture goes and another one comes, and building or destroying, the core of soul, spirit or character that protests evil and creates beauty will not be eradicated. That is why the painting is called 'The Landscape that Gives Hope.'"

Valentin had been a successful stage designer for the Leningrad film industry and a member of the Artists Union, worked long hours and liked it, and was possibly on his way to being great. In the late sixties, however, he came to realize that he was being given little chance to do anything of his own, so he resigned as designer, took a studio under union auspices, and became an "independent artist" within the union. He was still very productive but by the early seventies he could not escape the realization that the union was exercising subtle but effective pressure on him in the direction of socialist realism.

He made an appointment with the union chief, laid his union card on the table and walked out. He knew that shortly they would take his studio away so he gave it to a union member friend, and walked away from that, too.

All this was before the Tovarishchestvo existed, at a time in the Soviet Union when there was no real support or possibility to show outside the union. Valentin found a job designing posters, and began to use office equipment after hours to make his prints.

"If one of my Russian friends had asked me why I work the way I do, I would answer the question with another question: Why does a bird sing? But when you ask me, Barbara, I think that I shouldn't joke because the question is very serious.

"I operate from the idea that creators and artists are chosen by God. *Any* human being is happy to be alive, you know, even the most punished soul on earth, even a person dirty from troubles and bad times. Our lives are given from happiness, and only once, and that is why each one of us, one way or another, tries to express his feelings about life.

"But an artist is given, in a way, two lives: the external life that surrounds him, in which he lives each day, and the personal world that lives inside him. If he has been given the resources to pass that life on to others, then he is happy twice. I think that is the main motive for art of any artist. It is worth very little to copy correctly what you see, you need to also have your own feelings toward it. Those feelings come out in your art."

We were talking in the apartment of a friend who lives on Nevsky Prospect. Heavy maroon curtains and tiers of houseplants muffled the roar of the buses as they pulled away from the curb below. Tea steamed invitingly in delicate flowered cups. Valentin passed me a plate of homemade cookies. He has intense blue eyes with laugh lines, thick brown hair closely cropped, short curly bangs. He is compact and athletic and bounces when he walks.

I gazed at a piece of his work on the friend's wall. It was only fourteen by fifteen inches, delicate yet with bold contrasts of black and beige, red and hunter's green. A magpie stood outside his cage looking toward the daylight. The cage resembled a destroyed church. On the green table in front sat a jar with a paintbrush, through the window to the right a boatman poled his skiff. Two enigmatic birdlike cloths stood below the window, poised for flight as was the magpie. I raised my eyebrows questioningly.

"It is a nostalgic piece also. I call it 'In Memory of Gregory Sorokin.' It contains three copies of paintings by the artist Sorokin, a destroyed church as a symbol of this departed culture, and a magpie, a 'soroka.'

"In the 19th century, an artist apprenticed a very talented serf, Gregory Sorokin. All his life, Sorokin painted landscapes for the nobleman on the estate where he lived. They are piercing, pure, transparent; the people in them are holy—I can find no other word. You would never say that someone who was a serf drew them: a free man drew them, as an artist should be.

"But when Sorokin was finally given his freedom he began defending the rights of those weaker than himself. An artist like him could not act otherwise; from his paintings you can see how deeply he loved and how close he felt to the world outside him. He came into conflict with the authorities and they sentenced him to a beating with birch twigs. They did not have such interesting punishments in those days. Not being able to wait for such shame, Sorokin hung himself.

"How sad these memories are," Valentin tapped on the table with his fingers. The street outside had darkened and lights had come on in the building across the street. "I did not invent any of this."

14 . EVEN A LITTLE HOUSE

lyona, Sergei and I spent my last day in Leningrad
together. After breakfast at their apartment we took
buses across town to the basement club where Alyona
and some members of her hand-weavers' group teach
in an after-school program. The equipment is minimal, a few
small standing looms and some inexpensive table models with
narrow beds. Since the club is supposed to be for the students,
the staff can't tie up the looms long with their own creative
projects, but they use them when they can in off-hours.

"I work as an accountant," Alyona had told me, "just doing

Alex Kan and the author in the studio of Anatoly Belkin.

Poster for the controversial Spring '86 TEII exhibit. The black stroke signifies cancellation by the Department of Culture. The unofficial artists added the red.

Sergei Kovalskii in his studio-apartment.

Kovalskii's "Breathing is Forbidden," one of the pieces the censoring committee wanted removed from the Spring '86 show. (photo: Martin Zeitman)

Arkady Dragomoshchenko, poet, with Timur Novikov, leader of a fractious group of young artists, the New Wilds. They now call themselves simply the New Artists.

The workspace of Yulia Ivanova. Every artist seemed to have a skull somewhere in the studio.

Farewell party, December 1986, in Sergei and Alyona's apartment.
L. to R.—Yul Rybakov, Elena Figurina, Alyona, Sergei, and the author.

Yul Rybakov and two parts of his triptych, "Once Upon a Time There Lived...."
Yul had to carry the painting to a neighbors to see the triptych whole.

In "The Landscape That Gives Hope" Valentin Gerasimenko contrasts "spiritual Old Petersburg with the faceless monster of New Leningrad."
(photo: Martin Zeitman)

Gerasimenko and Zhenya Tykotskii prepare to chop down a bothersome tree in the dead of night.

*Lenina Nikitina with her paintings in the courtyard of her apartment building.
(photographer unknown)*

*"Corpses," one of Nikitina's memories of the Nazi's 900-days
siege of Leningrad, in which she lost her entire family.*

Lyuba and Alyosha's dacha forty minutes north of Leningrad.

Sergei, New Year's Eve 1987–88.

Elena Figurina's self portrait, 1985.

Figurina after the opening of a personal exhibition in the Aurora Publishing House, Leningrad 1990.

stupid things with numbers. To me, it's much more interesting to talk about weaving or movies or books. If I could get a hundred rubles a month for doing weaving, I would leave all those economics to hell. I think I will anyway—why spend so much time doing something you do not like at all? I think that after this year I will be working somewhere else. I don't know where, maybe with kids."

Shortly after my arrival a few weeks ago Alyona's handweaving group had a stand at a downtown fair, the first fair in many years where local craftspeople were allowed to display and sell their work. I had gone over late morning and watched as, bit by bit, a crowd gathered until the square was filled. People living in the apartments framing the square leaned out their windows and talked to their neighbors. A Fourth-of-July type uniformed band led a parade of mummers around the circle—a dragon, a chicken, a giraffe, a witch danced and bobbed with the children; a rock group and some breakdancers performed.

Sergei and Alyona had built a stand from which the weavers hung their tapestries; they strung the woven belts and ties and laces over the park bench and sat on stools talking and joking with each other. I offered a little capitalistic advice—if they really wanted to sell anything they should pay some attention to the people looking at their work: look at them, talk to them, give them a chance to ask questions—but the weavers stared at me a little bleakly. "We don't really care about selling anything," Alyona explained, laughing. "We just want to exhibit and have a good time."

"How do you manage working full-time, doing the housework and being a weaver as well?" I asked Alyona as she, Sergei and I sat down at the table in her club. "Who takes charge of things at home, for instance?"

"What she means is, who decides when you go to the kitchen," Sergei said dryly to Alyona.

"Of course, Sergei and I decide everything together. What do you want to know concretely? Who washes the dishes?"

"Yes. You work, right? And he works. So when you come home at night, who goes shopping, makes the dinner, makes sure the laundry is done, takes care of the daily life?"

"I do all of this, of course," Alyona said. "Sergei sometimes helps me bring in something heavy from the store, or takes the laundry to the laundromat. He does the heavy male work, hammering something in, painting. He made the furniture in the kitchen, that sort of thing. But I cook. I like to cook when there is time, it's not a hardship at all, and when there is no time, he cooks for himself. He cooks wonderfully, he just always has very little time. He can make kasha, soup, omelets, everything."

"I can do a lot," Sergei grinned at us smugly.

"You can do everything!" said Alyona.

"It's just that there is never any time," he added, "but I try."

A scene from last week flashed to mind. Sergei had expected Alyona back from work around two in the afternoon, but she staggered in only at four, loaded with groceries. Sergei let fly at her. "Where have you been? You said you'd be home at two and it's already four. I'm hungry! We've had nothing to eat all day!" Alyona had set the groceries on the table. "Go back and sit down with Barbara," she ordered, "I'll fix you dinner right away." Sergei was still pouting twenty minutes later as he sat down to eat. Alyona put down the soup ladle and stood behind him. She began to stroke his head. "He's like a cat," she said to me. "Once you feed him and stroke him a little, he purrs." Sergei tried to look angry but a giggle escaped. He saw nothing incongruous, however, about his anger: she was late and he was hungry. "I come home late at night and she's asleep. I wake up in the morning and she's at work. So, nothing to eat all day long."

"Sergei is a very good person in this sense," Alyona continued, "very comfortable. He never says that something doesn't taste good, yuck, take it away! I try to cook well, but he is not very demanding. Everything is OK. He doesn't beat me if something doesn't come out well." She giggled. "But, seriously, I think that Soviet life can be really hard for women, especially women with children: you see them on the buses coming home at night and they are so tired. I don't think they should have to go to work."

"Do you want to have children, the two of you?" I asked.

"Yes," Alyona said.

"What, yes?" Sergei snapped to attention.

"I want to have children," she said.

"And you?" I turned to Sergei.

"No time. I have no time to think about it. That would change everything. Understand," he scratched his neck, "now I don't have to think about earning money. If I need something, I can go without it. But then, no, I would have to think about earning money and when could I paint, when could I do Tovarishchestvo work? I already have what amounts to three jobs: my work on the Tovarishchestvo, for which I don't get any money; my job, where I get very little money; and my creative work, where I also don't get any money, or rarely. And I write articles—a fourth job. So I have no time as it is, but the main thing is that I do not have to think about money. If there is none, okay, at least we have bread and butter."

"I think that Sergei says this because he is a very responsible person," Alyona said a bit wistfully. "If he takes something on, then he takes it on with whole responsibility. That is why he talks this way. I think that he likes children, and would like to have them. It is just that there's a lot we can't figure out."

"Like where, for example?" Sergei gestured hopelessly. "She is an artist and I am an artist. You have seen where we live and work. And if there were also children, one would go crazy. Even as it is there's no room to live."

"Let's go live in the village," Alyona said, "the village is good. There are cows...."

"We'll get a dog..." Sergei added.

"We'll walk for milk...." There was a silence. The two of them looked at each other quietly. I was touched, and sad, and realized how much I loved them both.

"How do you feel about living with so much of Sergei's art all around you?" I asked Alyona, thinking of the congested apartment. "It takes up so much room."

"The paintings don't bother me," she said, "I like them. His work is good." Sergei bowed formally. "But there is very little room. That bothers me. I would like a larger apartment, maybe even a little house," she turned to me. "It is *very* nice in the village."

"Maybe even a palace?" Sergei proposed.

"No really," Alyona said, "it is bad, but what can be done? Do you hear, Sergei? What's the matter?" Sergei was laughing. Alyona looked at him sharply. "You see," she spoke very firmly to me, "without the paintings, it is also lonely. But then, it's lonely without children, too. Such is the problem. We need to think and think. We need a studio for Sergei. I hope that we will have a studio *and* children."

"And there you see," said Sergei, "that's exactly why we organized our Tovarishchestvo—so that every artist could have a studio, exactly for that! So far, neither Yul nor I have the right, not even the possibility, to rent such a space, even if we find it."

"There should be a Tovarishchestvo which would provide studios and a decent upbringing for children," Alyona said, "so that everything would be normal for the artists—so that you could exist with children. We could unite and form a kindergarten of some kind."

We drifted off into talk of nursery schools and daycare problems, in Russia and America, and soon left to walk together. You could feel that spring had finally come. Clouds scudded through a pale sky. Friday's rain had cleared the sidewalk and, when we emerged from the dark of the club, the pavement had a warm yellow tinge in the patches of sun. We walked along the Moika River, over small curved bridges, under willows. The willows were brushed with lime-yellow and the grass was greening up. Ducks splashed in the brown water, muddy with the winter run-off, and pigeons fought over chunks of bread.

Sergei went off to work after early dinner in a cafe; Alyona and I played hopscotch in one of the games chalked on the sidewalk and walked until it became dark, close to ten, talking about friends, about books, about her dreams to see something of the world. I think Alyona is a very wise and beautiful woman, childlike and often effervescent in her enthusiasms but with a core of strength and grace. She follows contemporary Russian literature through the 'samisdat' publications and knows Faulkner and Updike and Thomas Pynchon, Kundera and Gunter Grass. She also goes to as many film festivals as she can and recalls plots, actors and directors with ease. "Don't you remember the scene where he tells her he has to leave?" I shake my head. "Really, you don't remember? And then she says...

"Paris! if I could only see it I know I would love it. I know all the places I would go. I know every street. And everything I would eat! Of course," she added considerately, "I'd love to see America, too, but Paris! I have always dreamed of going to Paris."

PART III

Late September – Late October

1987

15. THE LONG DARK CARPET

This hotel, the Moskva, could easily become my second favorite after the cozy Evropaiskaya. The Neva curves around to the left and ships slip quietly by. Across the street, gray and mysterious in the morning mist, is the Alexander Nevsky Cathedral. Many people pass through the gates into the church grounds. Trucks that look like a children's matchbox series, short, square and rattly, trundle along across the river under a big neon sign that says, "Glory to the Party of Lenin." Trams and trolleys screech and roar, crowds surge in and out of the metro station below. It is very noisy but each conveyance is a great convenience for me and well worth the clamor.

Today it is totally overcast; last night when I arrived it was raining hard. I had been unable to phone to find out if Sergei and Alyona would meet me at the station, yet there they were, not at all sure I was really coming, standing in the rain with chrysanthemums. They settled me in my hotel and we went off to their place: Sergei had bought a bottle of champagne; Alyona fixed an omelet, fish, tomatoes, pickles, tea, berries. They had just returned from their place in the country to be here for my arrival, and the guest bed in the kitchen was covered with drying "kalinkas," tiny cherrylike fruits they had picked just days ago.
I will be here in Leningrad for a week, then go with the Association for Humanistic Psychology delegation to Moscow and Tbilisi, Georgia, and back here again for another ten days after the AHP group leaves for home. Since this will be my second-to-last trip before the exchange show goes up in Point Reyes—we have scheduled it for next May—I am pressed to actually go home with some work in hand.

I was upset to find that someone from Deutsche Bank has been buying a lot of Tovarishchestvo work and has, according to Sergei, completely bought out Elena Figurina. Sergei says not to worry, she's painting more, but I am worrying: whose work is left? Can I ask for assurances from the artists that they'll save me the pieces I want? I kept waking up last night in waves of dread: will our exchange be pulled out from under us by banks and the like? If these artists are "discovered," will prices go up so that, if we do have to buy the paintings, we can't afford them? Will painting for the soul be replaced by putting out for the marketplace? Right now I am not in the best of spirits.

We have been agonizing over how to handle our exchange. Sitting around tea at Sergei and Alyona's that first night with Yul and Alex, going back and forth about whom to see, whether and what to buy, what to hold out for, and whether to keep looking for official help, Alex broke through the spiralling tension.

"Maybe we should wait until things are simpler," he suggested. "Things are changing here month by month. What was inconceivable last year is now taking place. Just a year ago the rock group, Aquarium, was unofficial and unrecorded, and now

108

it has a record out and is being given permission to go to the States. Why should you all race around making these complex arrangements to export this and bid for that, when in a few months it may be possible to do everything with just a signature on a paper?"

I had a wave of panic, a loss of direction and momentum. Alex's suggestion to put the show on hold forced me to come to a decision. If Marta Petrovna has not figured out how to export the work and if I can't get approval from the Ministry of Culture to get the work out on consignment, I will buy the paintings myself and hope to get expenses back with sales. I have enough money in the bank and I think this show is a worthwhile project. I have no idea whether Tovarishchestvo work will sell in America, and, as I'm not choosing paintings with sales in mind, I may be stuck forever with forty-two pieces of art from Leningrad. Maybe this is how people become collectors. But it's good work and I want people in the U.S. to get to know this group of artists.

▲ ▲ ▲

Yesterday afternoon I caught up with Mudrova. As I crossed the long dark carpet to her desk she looked as if she had never seen me before. I reintroduced myself.

"Yes, yes, I remember you. No, I haven't done anything about your project. Without the Artists Union it is impossible. It is an international matter and does not lie within my jurisdiction." She fiddled with her pen. "I wish you success." Subject closed.

▲ ▲ ▲

I am accompanying Oleg and Olya, the photographers who shepherded me around Moscow last December, to the artists' studios. I need good slides of each artist's work for the catalog, and in order to raise funds and find galleries in the U.S. in which to place the show. As I accompany the photography team I get a second look at everyone's work and can make some less pressured decisions about which pieces to ask for.

The other afternoon we went out to Sasha Gurevich's apartment. Sasha and his family live way past Sergei and Alyona's in a new district—new in that there are large clusters of recently built eight-story apartment buildings, and more being constructed. Piles of dirt, sand and rubble litter the built-up side of the road. On the other side stretch birch woods with some old wooden homes visible here and there. Probably these were suburban dachas until recently. This late afternoon people were walking their dogs in the woods; groups of boys ran and jumped on the sand piles. The access roads from the bus to the apartments were a mess, unpaved: we picked our way on muddy ridges between puddles, tightrope-walking on the curbs.

Sasha is slim, semitic, rosy-cheeked and shy. He slouches a bit in the way of boys who grew too tall too fast. His paintings are large and complex, his own blend of Bosch and Chagall, often on wood panels in icon style. He probably has thirty pieces in the two-bedroom apartment, accomplished, intuitive work: a fantasy land of the real and the unreal—his own family, old villages, churches, city scenes, peasants and soldiers. He says that the paintings grow as he paints them; I imagine him in a half-dream state while he works.

The painting I am most captured by is about four by four feet square and mostly in reds. In the background a city of onion-domed churches frames a window through which you can see a pastoral landscape. Moving up from the bottom is a host of saints and clowns, including Gurevich himself, Valentin, and other friends. At the top, under a full rainbow, Jesus slumps on a nonexistent cross.

"Sergei," I whispered, "Do you think we could get Sasha to write something about any paintings we take? Most Americans won't understand all the associations."

Sergei looked puzzled.

"Well, I don't understand them myself," I confessed.

"What's to explain?" he asked, scratching his head. "I don't understand. To me, it's all perfectly obvious."

I chose one of the smaller paintings for our show, and, if we can get help with shipping, the rainbow painting.

▲ ▲ ▲

Around seven in the evening Sergei, Yul and I slogged through a gray and grizzly rain to a former church where an auction was being held. It was not yet dark; everyone was scurrying home from work hunched under umbrellas. We were among the first to arrive—a strange looking group: Sergei, straight from furnace-tending, in his worn leather jacket and patched jeans; Yul, elegant and combed in a well fitting dark suit; and me, very American, in maroon low-heeled shoes and a Sherlock Holmes raincoat.

Featuring both official and unofficial art works, this auction was the first to be held in Leningrad in seventy years. It was a benefit for the Leningrad branch of the Fund Kultury, Raisa Gorbachev's arts organization that is trying to break the monopoly of the Artists Union. Since no one expected much competitive bidding, Sergei thought I might pick up something by the Orlovs, or by Yul, cheap, and have the work sent to America at Fund Kultury expense.

I was given a number in case I wanted to bid, and an interpreter. Since I understood more from Sergei and Yul's Russian than from her English, and since she inhibited our gossiping about the paintings and the procedure, I sent her away as courteously as I could. But the work was disappointingly dull, consisting by and large of sweet landscapes, setting suns, and, as Sergei ruefully says, little pots with little flowers. The participating Tovarishchestvo artists had not hung their best work. The only piece I liked at all was Zhenya Orlov's. Sergei was quite put out at my hesitations—he had gone to a lot of trouble to arrange for me, a foreigner, to be able to bid. I, on the other hand, can't put out limited cash reserves for second-rate work.

A dignitary of the Fund opened the event with a long self-congratulatory speech praising the work of the Fund and underscoring how significant an event was this first auction in seventy years. As capper to the oration and to symbolize the opening of the bidding, he ran a little flag up a little flagpole placed on the front table, pulling the string with two fingers. The flag was only about six inches long and the juxtaposition of the bombastic speech and the tiny flag struck us as so ludicrous we were crumpled up with laughter. People turned to stare at us.

The evening was very subdued, quite unlike the American auctions I have been to where feelings run high and people jump up and wave for attention, shout comments across the room, crack jokes. In America an auction evokes desperation, competition, anxiety. Here things moved quickly without dissension. The art was propped on an easel in front and whisked away if no one bid. Only the auctioneer spoke: he would call out the prices and the buyers waved their numbered cards. Probably a third of the work went back to the artists because no one met the starting price. Another third sold without competitive bidding.

I bought Zhenya Orlov's painting for a good price and we were both happy. I bid on Yul's painting as well to drive up the price, gambling on getting stuck with a painting I didn't like— but I knew Yul could use the money and hoped I could trade that painting back to him for part of the triptych he had showed me in April. The ruse worked: when we got up to 700 rubles I quit and the other bidder got the piece. I found out later that I had been bidding against the Museum of Religious History.

I had very tentatively asked Yul if we might have the triptych for our show. Given the stringencies of duties and rules, it would probably never return. "I expect that would be a big loss for you," I said.

"I already thought it over," Yul said. "I would like the triptych to go to America. It will probably be seen by more people there than it would here, things being what they are. If our show travels to various places throughout the States, that's what's most important to me—a chance for the piece to be seen."

I feel honored by Yul's trust, and excited to have something so fine and thought-provoking for the show.

▲ ▲ ▲

I woke this morning to a beautiful day, the second in a row —the first decent weather since spring, they say. After breakfast in the hotel I went across the street to the Alexander Nevsky Monastery and meandered past the wooded cemetery to the church. In a front corner a service was in progress, five singers and a priest, with four or five old women kneeling on the stone floor praying. Further back under one of the stained glass windows, the warm colored light streamed onto two open coffins, an elderly husband and wife. A couple in their early forties stood by, the husband comforting his wife who was trying not to cry. Friends were arriving with flowers.

Outside in the park local retirees kibitzed over chess matches. Gusts of wind were bringing down the leaves, and the rowan trees full of red berries swayed under the sun. One sort of tree has huge maple-like leaves, each leaf ten inches or more across; the colors are intense gold and green. People gather them as bouquets, and on the metro I spotted several young women wearing crowns of them, looking like the saints in Igor Orlov's paintings, or like Maxwell Parrish maidens.

I took the metro to the end of the line to visit Yulia Ivanova in the Kupchino district. Everyone was out buying flowers and vegetables and preserves from the women who come in from the suburbs to set up their stands. Fifty or more merchants had set up tables and were hawking everything from bread to crocheted afghans.

Yulia gathered me up and took me on the tram to her apartment. It smelled of cake. The arthritic Great Dane, Marcel, had finally been put to sleep during the summer but Roosevelt the regal cat stalked the studio and rubbed against our legs.

There were many new paintings. I had seen several of Yulia's city paintings in April at the Kino demonstration and told her how much I liked them. "Actually I like the still-lives better," she said, "but maybe I'm a little sensitive on the subject after my argument with Valentin."

It seems that at the four-man exhibit last November Valentin had remarked to Yulia that she should stop painting still-lives and stick to landscapes. "Still-lives are weak, women's work only. You should paint strong paintings like Elena Figurina and Barbara Hazard," he said. Yulia replied that she wouldn't think of telling *him* what he should or shouldn't paint, but Valentin insisted that he knew what he was talking about and that she should listen to him. When she complained about this to Sergei he didn't have the vaguest idea why she would be upset.

"They don't understand at all what we're talking about," Yulia said to me. "Listen to this." A curator here in town—it might even have been Valery—had proposed that she and Bob Koshelokov show together. She parodied the curator. "'Your work resembles his a lot,' he told me. 'If you would just paint some things a bit more like Bob's, a bit more avant-garde, I'd arrange the show.' I told him to go to hell.

"Avant-garde, whatever that means, is very big here now," she continued, "and everyone is trying to outdo each other, trying something new every week. It's not their own work, you know, from the soul." She laughed ruefully. "Well, maybe I'm just not an avant-garde person."

I was sitting on the sofa-bed with Roosevelt curled up in my lap to sleep. Yulia got out paper and ink and did several drawings of us, but was not pleased with them. "Well," she said, stuffing them away, "too avant-garde."

Yulia is letting me buy a pair of paintings for the show: one of Roosevelt and one of Marcel. "I'm not sure I'm ready to part with him at all, but maybe in the long run he will have a better fate in the U.S. than here. People there may appreciate him more."

There is a possibility Yulia will be assigned a studio by the union. Although it has already taken much waiting in offices and filling out of forms, she is high on the list. I assume this is possible because she has academic training and works as a children's art teacher under union auspices. If she does receive a studio, she will be the first of our group to do so. Maybe the union is loosening up a bit.

▲ ▲ ▲

After so many initial doubts and hesitations, things are looking up again for the show. Elena has found out about an agency in Moscow, the Polyanka, that will pack and ship art out of the country. I called them from here: no problem, the man said, in English even, I can bring in whatever pieces I want to buy whenever I get to Moscow. I don't need elaborate documentation, simply the names of the artists; unofficial artists are fine; a painting the size of Yul's triptych is not too big. It seems too good to be true. Perhaps they will even take credit cards.

We will go to Moscow later this week, so we are now racing around Leningrad not only photographing but collecting the more unwieldy, uncarriable work we want for the show: Yul's triptych, two of Sergei's collaged paintings, and, now that someone will crate and ship it, Gurevich's "Rainbow." We are also taking two raw and bloody pictures by Slava Afonichev hoping that censors in Moscow will be more open-minded than those in Leningrad.

16 . A NOT UNCOMMON STORY

*E*arly morning on the train to Moscow is always quieting. Today a low mist clings to the ground. Streaks of deep orange border the horizon. We pass small gray lakes with a skim of ice near shore and men fishing. The leaves are now off the birches and the marshes brown, but the grass is still intensely green. I had somehow expected all Russia to be flat but hills and hummocks and rhythms of birch forests and fields swish past.

In the villages we pass train platforms with bundled up commuters. Men and women in padded jackets wait at crossings or carry bundles along dirt paths parallel to the tracks. Some are on bikes; motor vehicles seem rare. Small unpainted wooden houses, straw-covered gardens, outhouses, roof-high stacks of split wood flash by. As we near Moscow I begin to see some factory buildings and occasional three- or four-story apartment houses.

Generations of war dead lie here. It is hard to traverse this country, so easy and comfortable in this compartment, without imagining the soldiers—Russian, Swedish, German, French—slogging through the swamps dragging cannon and food supplies, cutting swaths through the birches with axes or tanks, looking for dry places to sleep or for something to wrap around their frozen feet. It makes me wonder about the skulls I see in every studio.

▲ ▲ ▲

As soon as I arrived at the station, Yul, Sergei, Elena and I gathered up the eight large paintings from the checkroom to take them over to the Polyanka office for export. Elena had brought Afonichev's work when she came from Leningrad on Thursday; Sergei, Alyona and Yul had brought the rest of the work on the night train Saturday. Gurevich's rainbow painting is bulky and heavy; Afonichev's large stretched piece and Yul's triptych, rolled, are both over five feet long. Yul stepped into the street and started trying to hail trucks, vans, off-duty buses, even a military transport, anything that might hold us and all this stuff. It was raw and windy and after half-an-hour we gave up on finding a truck and headed for the metro.

As we entered the metro lobby Yul leaned over me. "Barbara," he said quietly, "you must go and ask the guard a question. Get her to look in the other direction while we go through the turnstiles with the work. They don't like it when you take such big things on the trains, especially at rush hour, and they might forbid it."

The attendant turned to the wall map pointing out where I should "change trains," and as the paintings disappeared down the escalator I thanked her and went down the ramp myself.

Moscow and Leningrad subways are carved deep into the ground, perhaps six or seven stories down. Some say it is so they can be used as bombshelters, others simply that such depth is required to go below the swampy surface soil. It can be dizzying to look down. Although the escalators move at twice the speed of American escalators, a trip to the platform can take two minutes. It is a pause in activity, a time for contemplation of faces. Couples stand, the taller on the step below, and converse or caress each other. Others read or stare into space, or fidget impatiently.

It was still rush hour and trains were crowded. People had to squeeze past our paintings to get in and out and stared at us crossly, but we eventually emerged directly across the street from the building we sought. A former church turned office building, elaborate red brick with boarded up windows, it was now filled with thousands of pieces of artwork awaiting certification, payment or packing.

Elena guided me through the baffling paperwork in the office. Her brow knit as she puzzled over the forms and tried to figure out how to explain them to me. Every time the Polyanka staff left the office for a minute she would crack a joke or give me a little advice: "Tell them you absolutely have to have this by December," she said, "otherwise it will take forever."

I poked around the stacks of paintings waiting to be shipped while Elena, Yul and Sergei filled out forms for themselves and the others. There in a corner were the paintings by Elena I had wanted to buy, and work by Bob Koshelyokov, Gennady Zubkov, Oleg Kotel'nikov and others from Leningrad. It's already beginning, I thought, the skimming off of work from Leningrad. I felt a mixture of competitiveness and sadness: wishing I myself could afford to buy all the paintings that I love; angry that, since the artists have no idea what their art is worth, they are probably selling for absolutely nothing; and sad that the work must leave the Soviet Union to be appreciated. The Russian Museum should be collecting it instead.

Shipping through the Polyanka is not without its pitfalls. The buyer agrees on a price with the artist and the Polyanka adds an extra 24% for crating, shipping and export duty. However, a commission which meets only every ten days or so reviews the prices to be sure they are fair to the artist. The higher the price the more lucrative the Polyanka's 24%. I am to call from Leningrad in two weeks to find out how much I must pay. How to pay is not clear. They do not take Visa.

▲ ▲ ▲

This morning I practically forced Litvinov of the Ministry of Culture to talk to me, hoping one last time to get some official sanction for our exchange. All I *really* want is someone's blessing—the show will take place with or without it, for I am resigned to buying the work; it will not look good if I have to say that we tried for over a year to get approval for this gesture of goodwill and were refused.

"Look at this stack of papers!" Litvinov exclaimed, pointing to an eighteen-inch pile on his desk. "These are all requests for exchanges from large public organizations, The Guggenheim, The Smithsonian Institute. We are overwhelmed. I cannot help you. You should go to the House of Friendship." I just shook my head. Administratively, we have reached dead end.

▲ ▲ ▲

Now that we have no help forthcoming, we are left with three ways to export art: this new avenue, the Polyanka, is one: managed by the Ministry of Culture, it is, I gather, another facet of the attempt to by-pass the Artists Union's stranglehold on art export and bring in some hard currency. Not bad, if it really works.

The second way, the way I bought Elena and Valentin's work in April, through the Hermitage extension on Yakubovich Street, has the drawback of 100% duty on any purchase. The third way we will try when I return to Leningrad: the Lavka shop, a storefront enterprise set up by the union, will now process non-union art sales for a 7% tariff. However the Lavka "assessment" committee, a team of union members, has its own aesthetic and may reject work not meeting its standards. That is why we brought the gory Afonichev painting to Moscow with us. An additional drawback to the Hermitage and the Lavka is that I have to carry the work out of the country myself.

▲ ▲ ▲

Many of the artists from Leningrad have come to Moscow for the first-ever Chagall show, currently at the Pushkin Museum. Yul and Sergei waited in line outside the museum for three hours on Sunday to buy tickets, and when I passed by yesterday afternoon the line for the ticket booth stretched around the block. Coming to Moscow from Leningrad to see art is like travelling from San Francisco to Los Angeles, or from Boston to Washington, but the art hunger is so great and the times so exciting that Moscow is full of artists come from all over.

It is not only Chagall that is showing, for a new cooperative gallery on the outskirts of town is showing work from the fifties and sixties, including some of the now-famous emigres— Chemiakin, Ernst Neisvestny, and others—and at the palatial New Tretyakov Gallery is a show of work by Aristarkh Lentulov. Born in the 1880s and deeply influenced by Russian Orthodoxy, Lentulov was an influential member of the avant-garde movement. Until now it has been impossible to see his paintings anywhere in the Soviet Union, although his work hangs in museums all over Europe. His canvases done between 1910 and the early thirties are vibrant Cezannish-Cubist urban landscapes in singing flame and rose colors, ochres and cedar greens. Onion-domed churches roll into the hills, rust-colored streets careen between gold and orange buildings. Then, as we went deeper into the exhibit, something happened: the work flattened, lost its spirit and began to imitate itself.

"Lentulov really believed in communism, in the hopes for a just society," Yul said, "but by the early thirties when Stalin's crackdowns began, he lost his hope. He had to keep painting, he was too much an artist to stop, but, not being able to fully express himself, this is the result. It is, unfortunately, a not uncommon story."

17. GRAY, SUNSET AND FAMINE

*B*ack in Leningrad, I have been making the rounds again of the artists' studios. Zhenya Tykotskii paints in his ex-wife's apartment, a large room in a communal apartment which he uses while she's at work. Tykotskii is appealing: tall and beanpole thin, balding, Jewish, intense, missing all but a few front teeth. He likes to tell stories and asks questions in an urgent confidential manner. He smokes urgently too, holding the butt between thumb and forefinger, stabbing it at the ashtray or the listener.

It was Tykotskii who had done the etchings of Jewish families that so moved me in the November four-man show. I had lost some sleep over him worrying that the KGB, having confiscated my journal, now knew he used the union presses in Moscow. But there seem to have been no untoward consequences. Tykotskii is now, however, concentrating on painting. His recently completed series is quite soft, in blues and aquas, grays and pinks, usually with one or two simple figures—a mother and child, a couple, a child and a bird, often touching each other. These paintings could easily have crossed over into sappiness but have not. Tykotskii's ability to handle paint and his close observation of the particular have kept him clear of sentimentality. Currently he paints mostly in black, gray and white: people with double faces, flat drawing merging into modeled images, two-dimensional people stepping on lifelike shadows. I chose one of these new pieces for the show, and two more prints.

I had first gotten to know Tykotskii a bit one night when Valentin and Tanya invited me for dinner. There was a plan afoot: the trees by their windows had grown so large that in summer no sun at all reached the apartment. To receive official permission to cut down a tree requires canvassing neighbors on both sides and five stories up, and then wading through several levels of bureaucratic decisions. The alternative is the axe at night. Zhenya Tykotskii arrived with his axe.

"We'll wait until after nine o'clock," Valentin explained over supper. "That way everyone in the building will be listening to the evening news and be less likely to interfere with us."

Tykotskii is very tall and wears a light blue knit stocking cap with a point. Valentin is short; his cap is navy blue and fits tight on his head. They both wear dark jackets. As Tanya and I watched through the kitchen window all we could see was Tykotskii's cap rhythmically swinging with the strokes of the axe.

Just as they picked up the second tree to haul it away, two militia men sauntered around the corner and came over to inspect. "Citizens, are you with the Commission?" one of them asked.

"Yes, indeed," answered Valentin. He and Zhenya hoisted the tree they had just cut onto their shoulders and set off purposefully into the dark. That seemed to satisfy the militia who went off down the path talking to each other, but Valentin and

Zhenya quit and came in for a drink. Valentin went out later and rubbed mud on the stumps so they wouldn't be too visible.

▲ ▲ ▲

One afternoon I hopped a bus with Valery Shalabin and rode out to his apartment. Valery is one of the few people I can talk to in English; he follows the art scene and is full of stories and morose good humor. The bus shuddered its way over the river and turned north along the eastern side of the embankment. The wind had come up and a fine rain enveloped us. We got out across from an elegant cathedral, turquoise etched with eggshell trim, four onion-domed towers on top and another marking each corner of the walled grounds.

"That's the Smolny," Valery said, "built by Rastrelli, the famous Russian architect of Italian origin. I think my window faces on one of the most beautiful places in Leningrad. Usually people look out onto noisy streets or dirty backyards; for me, facing the wall of some building or some dirty place would be torture." Valery led me behind a large building and into a tiny elevator. The doors slammed and the cage rattled upwards. It smelled of urine. We walked down the dark hall and Valery unlocked his door. Light from the gray river poured into the narrow room. The cathedral beyond was surrounded by the rust and black of wet autumn trees. Four stories below, the din was deafening; six lanes of buses and trucks roared in and out of the city.

"Looking out this window, it would be impossible not to become a painter," said Valery loudly. He had hung up our coats and come to stand beside me. His thick dark hair and beard came three inches below his shoulders, full and shiny. "Every day I see beautiful, striking sunsets here, all different. Many of my fellow artists accuse me of using too bright colors in my paintings, but if they would look at these sunsets for a week or two, I think it would be hard for them to use such dark colors themselves."

Valery's easel stood near the window, a paint-encrusted palette on the sill. Newspapers protected the floor. The walls were covered with abstractions in deep blues, oranges and reds. I will not include Valery in the show, although I have become very fond of him, for I think that his work needs a few more years of exploration. He paints a lot now, in spite of a full-time job at a small museum.

"My wife and I live in comparatively good conditions, you know," Valery said, sensing my awareness of his crowded room. "We have just the one room and kitchen but at least it is not a communal apartment; I have no neighbors to tell me to stop producing this smell or to keep my paintings out of the corridor.

"It is sometimes hard for my wife to coexist with these big canvases and brushes and fresh paint everywhere, but she understands me well; she is my most severe critic, but she likes my paintings. It's hard for me, too, living with my work around me all the time: the smell! Sometimes I need to think about something else, which is impossible with all these unfinished canvases around, so we get away to Anna's parents. We just go and live with them for a few days.

"This room functions as bedroom, dining room, studio, hotel for friends and guests. It's also an office, and sometimes a dance hall."

Valery brought in some tea and cake. "How did you come to be an artist?" I asked. "Were you trained in an institute?"

"It's always hard to answer how I managed this. I got some training in the House of Pioneers—the children's organization. But when I got to the university it was clear that the sort of art I was interested in was not what they were teaching, so I decided to become a historian instead. Then I was going to be an archeologist, but during expeditions I kept getting more and more visual information and four or five years ago I decided to stop all research work and become a painter.

"It was very important to realize that I wasn't alone, that others were interested in the kind of art that interested me—abstract art, expressionism, surrealism.

"I never had to break away from socialist realism because I was never addicted to it at all. Everything I saw at official exhibitions was very dull. The Artists Union is only interested in preserving their style, and preserving the money they get from the state for their canvases. The situation is funny because no real people buy that stuff—the Artists Union people just buy it from themselves: they make it, they set the cost, they buy it and then stuff it away somewhere. Nobody needs it.

"Things are changing a bit in the Ministry of Culture now, though. They are beginning to show some of the old Russian modernists—you saw Lentulov in Moscow—but in the union, even though they make speeches about how good it is to show everything, to see everything, practically speaking they are against anything new. They have their position in the sun and they don't want to lose it."

▲ ▲ ▲

Later in the afternoon, Valery and I went for a second look at the work of Lenina Nikitina. I had met her in April after the Dom Kino street protest. One of the older generation in the Tovarish-chestvo, a small, stocky, gray-haired woman, Lenina was born in 1931, the same year as me.

Lenina lives in a Dostoevskian yellow building near the center of town up a staircase off a courtyard of drains and rubble. The stairs are worn, waterstained and barely lit. Raskolnikov lurks on the landings. You enter the apartment through a dark kitchen that has absorbed generations of questionable sausage, and hang your coat in a narrow hall leading to the small studio-bedroom. Lenina has built a loft over this hall where she stores her paintings.

Like many of the artists, she paints in various styles: flat-color religious paintings, watercolor abstractions, drawings of kittens, an oil self-portrait. But I had been haunted by some pieces I had seen in the spring—Lenina's memories of the World War II Blockade.

Lenina painted this series in the early seventies on the Russian equivalent of masonite. In one, a cloaked woman kneels with hand outstretched to another woman, pleading. The second woman lays her empty hands palms up on the table. There is nothing to give. Behind them both, half hidden in the dark background, a third woman, cadaverous, leans her head on her hand and, watching, listens to some faraway music. The title is "Famine." In another painting, "But We Have to Eat," a young girl watches as her mother raises an axe over the neck of the scrawny family cat. "Corpses," is an ochre and gray study of hooded women carrying a wrapped body on a stretcher. The tight vertical and horizontal composition keeps any hint of bathos at bay.

"It would be hard for me to see these go," Lenina said. "This series is a requiem for my family. I was ten years old when the war began. My father had already died; I lived in Leningrad with my mother and sister. They both died of starvation. All these impressions, this heavy childhood, just lived in my soul and sought some kind of exit. As soon as I had the strength and skill to do so, I told the story as best I could through my art." Lenina thought for a minute. The mama cat who had been nursing her kittens in a box in the corner got up and stretched and a kitten dropped from a teat.

"People here have seen them," Lenina continued. "Maybe it is time for them to come to your country so people there will know these things about war."

"It is what we would like," I said. "We are not organizing this art show to raise money, but as a gesture of peace. We would write about these paintings so that people know what they are about and what they mean to you. But I don't want you to part with them if it will be too hard."

"No, I have decided," Lenina said. "Please take them. Let them be my word of peace. I want our nations never to fight each other and never to do harm to each other. Any war brings with it uncountable hardships, often quite unexpected and unimaginable. Let them go to America. But you are not to pay for them. They are not for money."

Lenina will let us have two paintings in December, "Famine," and "Corpses." She will try, she says, to make herself copies before she lets them go. Technically, we might be better off with the copies since the originals are painted over other paintings—again, the difficulties of obtaining canvas and stretchers—but it seems important to show the originals into which went so much history and pain.

1 8 .   F I F T Y – F I F T Y

"**Y**ou are trying to set up special conditions for women," Yul addressed me very firmly. "I think there should be as many women in your show as we really have here in art—if they are 70%, fine, if 50% fine." Gallery Route One's request that half of the participants in the show be women had come up once again. We had just finished reading together an article I had written about the Tovarishchestvo, and I had mentioned our trouble finding enough strong women artists.

I was already in trouble with the group because of some things I had said. I had known I was playing with fire when I asked Valery to translate and read my article aloud, but I needed to know if I was absorbing correctly what I had been seeing and hearing among the artists. I also wanted not to rely only on Sergei as consultant but to keep the relationship with the group as a whole.

This evening the table at Galia and Zhenya Orlov's had been opened up once more. The red and white plaid cloth was covered with heaps of salad, ratatouille, bread and cheeses. Zhenya had uncapped a frosty bottle of vodka and poured it into tiny shot glasses. Galia brought in a bowl of steaming potatoes and some pickled mushrooms. Everybody dug in.

More than the usual crowd had gathered: Sergei, Yul, Valentin, Valery, Zhenya's younger brother Igor. Sasha Gurevich had joined us, Elena Figurina as the only woman artist, and a couple of the artists' wives.

During Valery's reading there had been a great deal of knee slapping, exclamation, argument, conspiratorial winks, and whispers behind hands. Sergei and Elena joked with each other at the far end of the table. I had gotten some words wrong and was corrected, but a more serious infraction had to do with a quote— I swear it was a direct quote—from Yul. "Yul says he wants to stay out of trouble," I had written. I might as well have called him a coward.

"I think that you will never be able to understand Yul's deed. That is why you wrote that he has become more careful. You see," Valentin said, "Yul is the sort of person who will continue to express his social views—not in such boyish gestures as writing on walls—but with new steps of more significance. He has simply become more wise. He may stay in trouble, but in a more productive way. That's the sort of person Yul is."

I had not meant to imply that Yul was not continuing to act on his principles and I said so, but we became involved in a long and fruitless argument about semantics.

"Never mind," Valentin said. "It's good that you read this to us. This article helps us to reach your essence. Until now I thought, well, that you were a nice person to have a drink with, to eat dinner with, okay? But now I see that we have more agreements than disagreements—I'm talking about some psychological, human things, beyond language."

He turned to the group. "Usually, when we artists get together we don't talk so seriously. We make everything into a joke and don't allow ourselves serious discussions—maybe we belong to the class of people who joke about their illnesses, who knows? So Barbara has given us a chance to talk more deeply with each other." He paused a minute. "So there, Valery, translate all this nonsense, will you?"

Yul had at last brought the conversation around to my difficulty finding strong women artists. Whether something was made by a man or a woman might be a burning issue in America, he suggested, but in the USSR it was not.

I argued: given that fifty percent of the people on earth are women, it seemed reasonable to me to request that, when we are proposing an art show, fifty percent of the artists be women. The fact that it has been very hard to find even ten strong women artists in a city as large and cultured as Leningrad has, if nothing else, raised the question of why there are not more. It seemed like an important question to raise.

Valery translated and then added sotto voce, "That's not my opinion, you guys, but I'm only the translator and all of you can go to hell!"

Elena had been sitting quietly at the far end of the table near Sergei. Now she leaned forward, holding her hair off her forehead with her right hand, and objected. "The American gallery is opening a door for women. They're saying, 'Come on, let's do something to change the situation....'"

Yul bristled. "One would think you felt some sort of discrimination," he said to Elena. "Why are you so interested in this and why is it important?"

"I *do* feel discrimination," Elena returned, "from the artists themselves."

"What are you talking about?" asked Yul. "You and the other women who come to the Tovarishchestvo are in a privileged position, understand?"

"You are a male artist but I am a woman. Everywhere I run into the point of view that a woman does not have what it takes to be an artist. Sure, you give us a hand down out of the bus, but...." Elena began. She shrugged.

A flood of thoughts diverted my attention. I have been touched by how tenderly these men watch out for me. They get off the bus first and reach a hand back to help. They hold my elbow if the ground is slippery, and my hand going through crowds. They carry my bag, always weighed down with camera and tape recording equipment, and take my coat to the cloakroom. I am unused to these attentions after years of stateside liberation and, up to a certain point, I like them, but I have also been aware of the many evenings when I, the star, the foreigner, sit and talk with the men while the women work in the kitchen. This evening is another such. Were I not the American would I be in the kitchen myself? Even if I was one of their best artists? Would I be heard as an equal or condescended to? Flirted with, or ignored?

Zhenya Orlov tried to smooth things over. A woman artist must combat the myth of Man the Creator and The Woman Who Helps Him, he was saying, but if she can come through this and apply to the Tovarishchestvo, she receives much more attention than even the most talented man.

"Very bad, Zhenya!" Elena wagged her finger at him and turned to the others. "See, this very attempt to be chivalrous is the reverse side of discrimination against women. It is really insulting. A woman simply cannot overcome these stereotypes!"

"Don't get all worked up!" Valery said. "Come on. You overcame them. This is typical women's hysteria; I see no conditions of deprivation for women artists. This fifty-fifty requirement assumes that women are *a priori* considered to be weaker artists and must be given easier conditions. Real democracy," he added, turning to me, "is letting things be as they are. Perhaps in America you don't understand that."

Everybody jumped into the fray.

"I think you should evaluate an artist with artistic standards only," Valentin said stolidly. He was sitting back in his chair arms folded tight across his chest. "We are not talking about feminists but about artists. There should not be a difference between a male and a female artist, although God knows it often exists. There *is* a biological difference: there are areas where women are twenty points ahead and areas where they are six behind. You cannot get away from that. It is a fact of nature."

"Most modern feminists reject this given," said Valery gloomily. He had totally abandoned his role as interpreter. "You are trying to solve some sort of social problem of women artists with this requirement, Barbara, while for us it is purely a problem of aesthetics."

I thought sardonically of the decision the Tovarishchestvo had made *not* to have the "twenty best artists" show in May—a decision hardly just based on artistic merit. What ever happened to that idea? I had asked them. They couldn't do it, Valentin had told me, they would have had to have a parallel show for all the other artists at the same time. Since they were only allowed one exhibition space at a time by the Department of Culture, they had to have the more democratic show. It would have been too cruel to the artists that had no other opportunity to show. The interests of the majority versus the interests of the few. The issue had hardly been decided on aesthetics alone.

I looked down the table at all my Leningrad colleagues. These issues of sexism are always tough, at home or away, and arguments are seldom productive, yet I found myself feeling privileged at being entrusted with an honest confrontation.

"Maybe the question is this," I ventured slowly. "Really, if we were to say, 'twenty artists, it doesn't matter if they are men or women,' then it might turn out that you would send work of only two or three women..."

"Or maybe not a single one!" fired up Elena. "Just how many good women are there, in reality, in our Tovarishchestvo? Some strange arithmetic calculations, very artificial and naive are going on here."

"Okay, okay, calm down, *you* would be there. Just sit there and be quiet!" Valery continued with his translation.

"One of the hardest things," Elena interrupted, "is that a woman artist, even one whom you artists consider talented and privileged, still finds herself isolated. I have no, absolutely no, colleagues to talk to about art. Something is always assumed, and if it weren't for the fact that Barbara is here, I'll bet I wouldn't be sitting with the rest of you tonight either. You know that. There is no relationship to a woman as an artist; she's either a broad or a...."

"That's totally untrue," Yul said.

"It's true. I've experienced it in my own skin. How do *you* know how a woman lives? I don't have a single male friend with whom I can converse. Either his wife tears out my hair, or something quite different occurs. Do you know why I was so happy to participate on the Tovarishchestvo committee? Because it is my only chance to communicate with artists. I want that."

Some of the others had drifted out for a smoke and now Yul got up, too. The women were in the kitchen washing up and joking. Valentin remained at the table with Elena, Valery and me. "Art is composed of three elements," he said softly, "form, catharsis and ecstasy. In the long run, they occur differently in man and woman. It's purely biological, you see? You can't approach art with social measures, here or anywhere: there is simply the artist, that is enough."

"I don't know," said Elena shaking her head. "It just really works me up how clumsily we all approach problems. Including Yul."

We looked at our watches. It was already 12:20. We went out into the smoky hall and gathered up our coats. "I thought you understood less than you do," Elena said to me. "Now, having heard what you have written about us, I, like Valya, feel a direct connection with you. But," she raised her eyebrows, "I still haven't written *my* article for you to read, so you don't yet understand me. When I come to America, I will write it, okay?"

"That's a promise," I said, and we hugged each other.

▲　▲　▲

The next time Yul and Valentin saw Elena, they lit into her. "We have gone out of our way to be good to her," Yul told me afterward. "We have done so much for her, she is in no position to criticize us for our treatment of women." His voice had risen above its usual quiet tone. "And we can't understand why she would say all those things in front of a stranger. It's our internal business, not something that concerns outsiders. Anyway, I don't understand what she's talking about at all." Yul shrugged.

PART IV

December – January

1987 – 1988

1 9 .   C U L T U R A L   T H R E A D S

I had gone home to California for the month of November and was now back in Leningrad for three weeks over Christmas and New Year's to finish organizing the show. Rumors abound that export rules will soon change—we are pushing hard to buy the remaining work through the Artists Union Lavka commission before New Year's Eve—racing from studio to studio choosing pieces and lining up the artists for the Thursday export session.

The Lavka commission is much more wary than before. They have decided that I am a commercial dealer and so have raised the prices on some of the paintings—"These are charming, surely they are worth more than you propose." They refused altogether to allow me to buy five of the fifteen pieces. "These are not professionally done," the committee chairperson said, pointing to Sergei's "Forbidden to Enter" and Nikitina's blockade paintings. "We cannot allow them to represent Leningrad in America."

Sergei and I took the train to Moscow with the rejected paintings. The Polyanka promised to export them without delay, but then confessed that the paintings they were to have sent to me in November were still in Moscow. No one had tried to contact me about the delay and, had I not inquired, the shipment might have waited indefinitely. Some additional information is needed, they say, but they are not sure just what. I am to call next week from Leningrad to find out.

At the end of our day in Moscow Sergei and I went to see an exhibition of work from the 1920s—a magnificent show of Chagall, Malevich, Ulyanov, Rodchenko, Kandinsky, Filonov and others now being shown for the first time since the early 1930s.

The exhibition hall was still crowded even at eight o'clock at night. The catalog had sold out during the first weekend. The walls pulsated with color. People were talking about the work in hushed tones, quite unlike the atmosphere at a Tovarishchestvo exhibit. Paintings had been assembled from all over the USSR, from Smolensk, Krasnoyarsk, Novosibirsk—work that had perhaps originally been purchased by the union and sent to the sticks as part of the national send-the-art-to-the-people distribution.

Much of the avant-garde work left the USSR with the artists themselves in the '20s, as they migrated to Paris or Berlin or New York; some was taken out of the country by collectors like Armand Hammer or George Costakis. Some of the work, however, was hidden in the basements of the Hermitage, the Tretyakov and the Russian Museum by courageous curators, or not so courageous, as the case may be. Some work was preserved, often at some personal risk and great inconvenience, in private collections.

Pavel Filonov is a case in point. Filonov lived and worked in Leningrad and was acknowledged by his contemporaries to be one of the foremost artists of his day. His multi-figured, multi-faceted, often obsessive drawing-like paintings carry Cubism way beyond Braque and Picasso and anticipate the works of Mark Tobey and Fernand Leger. Filonov participated in a group show in 1927, and a personal exhibition was proposed and actually hung by the Russian Museum in 1929. But before the show could open, a barrage of anti-Filonov articles hit the press. The argument dragged on for two years, committees came and went, and in the end, the show never opened to the public.

Filonov died of cold and starvation during the first winter of the siege of Leningrad, 1941-1942, leaving vast quantities of work which had never been shown. His brother washed his hands of the whole matter, but his sister, Evdokia Nikolaevna Glebova, took all the work to her apartment—two rooms in a communal flat. As the war made it more and more imperative for residents to evacuate the city, she pleaded with the Russian Museum to store the work, at least temporarily. The museum agreed, but when, after the lifting of the blockade, she proposed that they keep the works as a gift, they declined. Everything returned to her two rooms over Nevsky Prospekt.

Every five years or so Glebova renewed her proposal to donate this great body of work to the museum and the museum again refused. Because Filonov had never had money for good art supplies, he had often painted on paper instead of on canvas. The paper began to deteriorate. Friends of Filonov and Glebova, Leningrad artists and restorers, tried to help conserve the works but without the equipment available only in the museums not much could be done. And still the Museum refused.

Towards the end of the Khrushchev era, a show of Filonov's work was organized in Novosibirsk, in central Siberia, three time zones east of Moscow. A Czechoslovakian art historian came to see the exhibit and, recognizing its extraordinary quality, photographed the works. From this issued, in the mid sixties, the first catalog ever of Filonov's work. Still the Russian Museum refused to show or to retain the collection. Only in the late sixties, thanks to the insistence of a young art historian, Evgeny Feodorich, did the museum begin to soften and at last accept the body of work.

They began to restore what they could. But until this moment, Filonov's work has never been shown. Rumor has it that a comprehensive exhibition has been scheduled for summer 1988 in Leningrad's Russian Museum. We shall see.

"Show me which artists had the most influence on you," I asked Sergei coming upon him in front of a Kandinsky. I have seen elements of many of the Russian avant-garde in his work: indeed, the two pieces that I chose for our show are entitled "Homage to Rodchenko" and "Homage to El Lissitsky."

We walked around together. "You know," he summed up, "it's not that I paint in the style of any of them, although sometimes I do a bit, but I have absorbed them into my heart, into my consciousness, and they have changed me inside. That has been my education as an artist—I never went to an institute nor took classes. These are the artists who have been my teachers."

I wondered as we circled the gallery one last time what the effect will be on contemporary Soviet artists when their own art history becomes available to them. I know that they have been familiar with images from reproductions printed in the West, but will being able to see the work itself free them not to have to continue to repeat that period themselves? What will come afterwards? Does ontogeny recapitulate phylogeny in the arts, or can one leap over great stages of development and arrive full blown in the late twentieth century?

▲ ▲ ▲

I had been talking about all this just the week before with Gennady Zubkov. I had gone to his studio to choose his pieces for the show. Gennady often shows with what some of the Tovarishchestvo scathingly call the Groupa Dollar: fourteen men who show together and have been selling for years to foreigners. Notwithstanding Tovarishchestvo snideness, Gennady is one of my favorite people in Leningrad; gentle and mischievous, a consistently good artist, seemingly not plagued by the pervasive Slavic melancholy.

The stairs to his studio were in terrible shape and the lights had been out for several weeks. Gennady had to lead me up the six flights by the hand. Light from the street barely illuminated the crumbling steps, railings were broken here and there, garbage overflowed the pails on the landings. The stair shaft stank. Gennady's studio, usually a model of order and beauty, was being remodeled by two artists from Alma Ata and the kitchen was an unbelievable pile-up of stuff. But in his workroom bread and sausage, toasted cheese sandwiches, apples and nuts waited on the table. Gennady hauled up a frosted bottle of vodka from a string attached to the window latch—"our refrigerator," he said.

We talked about the Tovarishchestvo show now on across the river from the Smolny Cathedral, about Gorbachev's visit to America and about our own work. Gennady keeps a photograph of one of my landscapes on the wall.

"You are lucky in the West," he said. "You know for us, in the thirties, the whole chain of development of our fine arts was broken. It has been very difficult to restore it. I was fortunate in that I got to work with an incredible teacher, Vladimir Sterligov. Sterligov tied together a lot of the problems of form and color that the avant-garde artists Matyushin and Malevich had been working on: how color influences form; how form influences color. Until then, artists had been interested in *either* color or form, either Impressionism or Cubism. Matyushin managed to combine the two problems into one. Thanks to Sterligov who tied it all together, I was able to touch on these problems. He was a live thread connecting the culture of the twenties and thirties with the *lack* of culture in the fifties and sixties. Because of him a whole generation of Leningrad artists had the chance to get to know about the avant-garde, the sources of our art in Russia and in the West.

"For our generation, next to the Russian avant-garde, I think, the greatest influence on us has been some of what went on in America in the sixties—Rauchenberg, Jasper Johns, pop-art, pop culture, new inspirations and new materials. They enriched all world art. They even got *me* fooling around with some new materials."

Glenn Miller's "Tuxedo Junction" engulfed us both in memories. Gennady poured the last of the vodka into our tiny glasses and we sat quietly for a moment listening. The building and the street were silent except for the sound of occasional footsteps from the frozen sidewalks. Somewhere in the distance a train wailed as a freight lumbered by, perhaps on its way north to Lake Ladoga and beyond, to Murmansk or Archangelsk and vast unpopulated regions now dark and covered with ice.

2 0 .   D A C H A   N E W   Y E A R ' S

New Year's Eve has absorbed much of the ritual formerly associated with Christmas and with earlier
pagan holidays. The tree, the tinsel, stars and snow-
flakes mix with goats and Siberian bears. Banners
flap across the streets, and window-writing and "Grandfather
Frosts" proclaim the turn of the year. People on the metro carry
bulky packages and spindly pines. Compared with American
Christmas hoopla, display is minimal, but holiday spirit is evident despite grumbling that the stores are empty.

I had managed, with dollars, to buy four bottles of champagne. Champagne has been unavailable to the general public for the whole two weeks before New Year's and everyone is furious, especially since there is not really a shortage; one hears that it will be back on the market mid-January and that this shortage is part of Gorbachev's anti-alcohol campaign. No one really knows, but people are outraged at not being able to drink the New Year in with the traditional bottle of champagne.

Sergei and Alyona had invited me to spend New Year's Eve in their friends' dacha in the suburbs. We had planned to leave the city in the early afternoon but, when I arrived at the apartment, Alyona was just beginning to cook. She had run out of flour for pies and was calling our hosts, Lyuba and Alyosha, to bring some over on their way out of town. Alyosha was having problems with their ancient car—it's older than he is, he says—but eventually it started and they appeared with the flour. They loaded up our gear and left for the dacha.

Alyona set me to work stuffing and crimping pilmeni, a sort of Siberian ravioli to be boiled and served in its own soup. Pilmeni is a traditional village winter dish. It is often made in large quantities and kept frozen in the snow. When needed, a hunk is chopped off with an axe and thrown into a pot. Hunters carry it on winter journeys.

Sergei, Alyona and I finally got underway at 8:00, pies in the basket, pilmeni in a daypack. The weather had changed. All December had been very mild, temperature in the twenties, light snow on top of sheets of slick ice. One day it even rained, and mini-avalanches of loosened ice fell from the roofs. Why people don't get killed I don't know. Maybe they do. I walk as far from the overhangs as possible. The sidewalks and the narrower streets get very slick yet everything is filthy. Instead of salt to melt the streets they spray sandy dirt, so one's boots are covered with mud. Everyone has been waiting for it to get colder, to snow a bit and get cleaner, and finally now on New Year's Eve day the temperature has plummeted. We stood on the train platform stomping our feet, exhaling steam with a crowd of similarly loaded down passengers. Sergei was grumbling about trains, about whether the bus would still be running, etc., but the train appeared, and then the bus, and at last slipping and sliding through the new snow, we plunged on foot down the hill towards the dacha.

The temperature was still dropping—the radio predicted -22° Centigrade [-12° Fahrenheit]—but the sky was sparkling. The road forked around clumps of small houses, became a path and then a trail, and we were alone slithering in the dark between lacy wooden fences and snow clotted berry vines. Occasional streams of golden light from an occupied house brushed the contours of the snow and silhouetted fruit trees and gardens humped with straw for the winter.

We staggered into the cabin around nine-thirty. Lyuba was busy in the kitchen getting things out of winter storage. Alyosha had brought out a carload of cardboard slabs, and he shanghaied Sergei to help carry them to the attic where they began to tack them to the floor for insulation. So far the only warmth was in the kitchen near the stove.

Alyona and I started a fire in the small fireplace in the front room and set up the tree. From a basket she pulled ornaments belonging to Sergei's family. It was a miscellaneous collection like mine at home—a few old glass Santas and faded peacocks, some newer cut tin and foil baubles, ceramic angels of awkward charm, all unified by lots of tinsel. I was touched that Sergei, who never speaks with fondness of his childhood, should have retrieved these treasures from his mother and, whether actively or through Alyona, arranged that they be the decorations on our tree.

Lyuba brought in salad and plates of hors d'oeuvres, and we placed our presents under the tree. At 11:30 we turned on the TV and started yelling with increasing urgency for the men to join us. Ten minutes before midnight they appeared, opened the first bottle of champagne, and we drank in the New Year. We put on our party hats and popped our poppers. Confetti exploded into the champagne and the salad. The salad had frozen by now anyway so we could hardly tell if we were eating cabbage or confetti.

We toasted our families, our futures, our friendships, our countries. An hour or so after salad Alyona brought in the pilmeni; an hour later, the apple and cabbage pirogi—thick-crust pies of yeast dough with Alyona's fancy braiding on top saying "1988".

The television, which usually virtuously shuts down at midnight, was broadcasting an all-night variety show: "A folk-singing group from Irkutsk greets the New Year!"; "The rock group Alyssa greets the New Year!"; "Alla Pugachyova greets the New Year!" MTV-like clips from contemporary rock groups followed one after another. Our conversation came to periodic stops when something worth watching would start.

I wondered, looking around the table at these young people, all between thirty and forty, the ages of my own children, how they had kept alive the traditions they observed—the gift-giving, the decorated tree, the toasts—and what they had lost. Before the Stalinist years of repression, had the turn of the year been a season of Christmas carols, decorations and traditional foods? Had the church played a role? Had they told fortunes at midnight? The television reflected none of this: the stage sets were strictly abstract. There was no "Silent Night" or even "White Christmas"; no "Christmas Carol" or "Nutcracker Ballet," and yet I knew that all over Leningrad my friends were gathering with those closest to them, were lighting candles on tinsel covered trees, and sensing a flow of time and tradition from sources deeper than ordinary knowledge. A stream may be blocked but the waters continue to flow.

We had pulled the table close to the fire and, still in our hats and coats, fed it tiny logs. The wood was green and burned slowly. It was very cold. Soviet authorities have been trying to discourage people from living full-time in these summer houses —God knows, maybe artists and other dangerous sorts might move out of town, beyond control. Maybe private home-ownership would become a rental business. To ensure compliance, there have been restrictions on the sorts of heating systems allowed, the sizes of fireplaces, and even on the amounts of firewood. Residents scavenge for wood at night and try to keep their wood piles hidden.

Lyuba's grandmother's house next door is old and lovely, Alyona had told me, a soft yellow with mullioned windows in the front room, a spacious downstairs and two bed-sitting rooms upstairs. Lyuba and Alyosha, however, building their own small house more recently, had diligently followed current code restrictions—only so many square meters per person, stove and fireplace of minimal dimensions. Now they are furious because the rules have relaxed and they could have built the house they really wanted.

Old Russia and New Russia, I thought as I shivered by the fire. Seventy years of suppression of taste, of choices, of anything one could call graciousness, in the name of equality and economy, to the point where a young couple building their own home have to nervously limit their dreams to such cramped utilitarianism. It seems a cruel idiocy that, when housing is so short in the city, people should be forbidden to live in the suburbs. Toksovo is at most forty minutes by train from the city.

"Have you ever been in such primitive conditions?" Alyosha worried. I had just come back inside from a trip behind the house. One thing about peeing in soft snow: it doesn't run into your shoes but sinks satisfyingly into the snow. Shit does too; it just melts its way underground. But at twenty-two below Centigrade you don't want to take long. "Do Americans have dachas like this? Built bit by bit out of scrounged materials? Without heat or plumbing?"

"Yes to all those questions," I said, "I have stayed in wood heated houses in Maine and in winter fishing boats in Alaska, but I never ate frozen salad before. It tastes just like confetti." He looked at me sternly and relaxed. We opened another bottle of champagne and exchanged presents. Alyona had bought me a Winnie-the-Pooh, "Vini Pukh" in Russia, and we exchanged records and scarves and socks. New Year's Day is also Alyona's birthday so we toasted her as well. Sergei put on his blue devil mask and Alyona her bird mask. I had rigged up my black knit cap with a beak and a crest. Sergei became increasingly expansive, pulling Alyona onto his lap, thumping on the table with his knife and fork. He rose to propose a toast and fell into the tea corner, breaking some cups.

At six o'clock we stumbled off to bed. By then the second bedroom had absorbed some warmth from the chimney and they moved a bed in for me with Sergei and Alyona. I had been afraid I would lie awake all night, or would have to get up to pee, but Vini Pukh and I slept till eleven, rolled around a bit and slept again till one.

Mid afternoon, already dusk, they got me on skis. It had warmed up a bit. We cruised through the village of small houses—some like Lyuba and Alyosha's constructed out of whatever came to hand, some, like that of Lyuba's grandmother next door, built long ago with second stories and porches and latticework windows. Many of the houses are painted intense yellows and blues. The lots, though small, are filled with fruit trees and shrubs; in summer they must be quite private and serene. The village is surrounded by wooded hills and lakes and the woods stretch quietly, softly, as far as one can see.

Sergei was in a very bad mood. Sullen. He hardly proffered a word all day except when we were skiing. Then he took tender care of me, coaching me, skiing on ahead and back again with encouragement. I had been using Alyona's skis and boots, and when Sergei and I returned to the house I suggested that she might want to go ski with him. Impossible, he said, her back hurts, and he went quickly off alone. He said practically nothing all evening but sat self-absorbed staring into the fire. Alyona looked very sad. Nobody had much energy for conversation. We heated up the leftovers from the night before and killed a bottle of vodka. Alyona and I went to bed around two but Sergei stayed up looking morosely at his feet or at the fire. "Are you feeling sad?" I asked Alyona and her eyes filled with tears. "Are you okay?"

"It's complicated," she answered.

▲　▲　▲

I came back to Leningrad alone around noon. Sergei and Alyona had offered to come with me but I knew they would never be ready to leave. When I woke Alyona to escort me to the bus, Sergei staggered up too, still grumpy, and insisted on coming along. The snow had melted from the branches and the roofs were dripping. Sergei pelted me with snowballs. The day was bright and the paths and hills alive with skiers out for the day. The bus was filled with folks returning to the city carrying luggage, skis, and sleds. As the bus rounded the corner I looked back through the window. Sergei and Alyona were trudging back down the lane, one behind the other, lost in their own thoughts.

21. THE TROUBLES COME TO A HEAD

When I entered Zhenya's shop in the slushy dark of a mid-January afternoon, three of the artists on the TEII council, the "soviet," were already crowded onto the sofa and eight others arranged themselves on assorted disintegrating chairs and stools. Sergei leaned stiffly against the wall. The tea kettle circulated. Everyone was smoking, but there was little of the usual banter as we waited to get down to business.

It had been with some apprehension that I asked Valentin if I might attend this meeting. Things have not been going well between Sergei and others in the Tovarishchestvo: Valentin is on the warpath, and Elena, too, and many of the others are fed up with Sergei's secretiveness and control. Bob Koshelokov has resigned from the soviet, or been fired, over some conflict with Sergei. Timur asks that Sergei not be middleman for any of our arrangements, and Valery spills over with gossip and resentments. Sergei will probably be confronted and perhaps asked to resign. Valentin thinks the whole committee needs to be replaced by younger members and, especially, that Sergei needs to step down. My guess is that he will never do it voluntarily.

"It's a matter of power," Valentin had said, shaking his head sadly. "It's very serious and very bad." For example, they are long overdue for an election of the soviet. Sergei, Yul, Valya, Elena, Zhenya Orlov, Afonichev, Vadim Voinov, Tykotskii, and, until recently, Bob Koshelokov—have been in office for five years. In 1985 all but maybe one had been reelected. Last summer when an election was scheduled, Sergei declined to call the meeting. Too busy, he said, the wrong time, too much in the works.

There had been a disagreement during jurying for the current Okhta Show in which Sergei objected to a ruling on the work of one young artist. Sergei got angry and said that what the jury committee thought was unimportant, that the committee was nothing anyway, and so forth. Valentin in protest withdrew his own pieces from the show. Sergei later apologized but Valentin mistrusts his apology. Yul suggests they tie the two of them up in a bag, throw it in the river, and let them fight their way out.

Elena, too, is disturbed by Sergei's high-handedness. He told her one day that if she continued to "go on like that" he wouldn't let her come to America. It was the first she had heard that we want her and Valentin to come for the show's opening.

▲ ▲ ▲

All this is disturbing on several counts. I am troubled to hear these things about Sergei, to whom I feel very close. I see now that it is more than having to work at a stupid job that is making him so ornery, and more than friction between him and Alyona. He can certainly be unpleasant and he does like to call the shots— I have never yet heard him admit to making a mistake—but after putting so much work into the Tovarishchestvo this must be deeply upsetting to him.

I spent the night at Sergei and Alyona's recently. Sergei was in a very bad mood. He received all the evening's phone calls with grimaces, groans, or lips clenched in annoyance, and stayed up till two o'clock drafting our accounts, sighing martyrishly and snapping at Alyona when she proposed he stand up for a minute so she could open the bed.

Alyona's situation at work has been contributing to the household tension. Someone "up above" ordered a cutback in staff—part of restructuring, eliminating the sinecures. The staff members that get kept on in this situation, Sergei says, are not necessarily the best workers: they are more apt to be the best friends, the relatives. Alyona's supervisor has been finding fault with her work and turning others against her. They have wanted her to quit voluntarily, but since there is an annual New Year's bonus she has been hanging on. Life at work has been miserable, she says: they have given her less and less to do and forbid her to either read or leave; she has had to simply sit at her desk doing nothing. She has been looking unhappy and getting sick a lot. Now that the bonus has come through she has given notice and is looking for other work.

The morning of my sleepover, Sergei waited to get up until Alyona had left. He went about organizing himself for work, slamming cupboard doors, wrenching pots onto the stove, smacking Alyona's book out of the way. When he sat down to his tea he said grimly, "You want to know why I work at this stupid job? It's just to keep from getting arrested, that's why. It's crazy." He stared furiously into his cup.

"Tell me when it's safe to speak to you," I said after a while. I needed somebody's phone number.

"Well, what?" he stopped dramatically in the middle of buttering his sandwich. I asked him for the number.

"On the train," he said shortly. Later, "Get your coat on." He walked on ahead quickly, suggesting a path but not offering a hand. I skittered after him on the ice.

On the commuter train he calmed down. "Listen," I said, "I know you're in a bad mood and don't want to talk, but I want you to know that when I get home this time I am going to need to hear from you. This is really our project, yours and mine. I have a committee but, like yours, they have other things to do and this isn't their first priority. You can't abandon me. I'm going to need moral support from you." I started to cry. "Oh, God," I said, "and it's only Monday. I don't leave till Saturday."

"Barbara, Barbara," he pulled me over and hugged and kissed me.

"You know," I continued, "we are not so different, you and I."

"Why? What?" he asked, surprised.

"Well, I think that only *I* can do things right, that others will mess up, not care enough. And besides, I can't stand to admit that I need help." He laughed, and then turned to stare out the window. We were passing through the train yard nearing the Finland Station. The snow had melted from the tops of the railroad cars and they steamed softly in the morning sun.

▲ ▲ ▲

The situation is a classic one. So often leaders get isolated with the work—no one else shoulders any responsibility. They take on more and more and get highhanded, believing that no one else can do it right or that there is no time to consult. They begin to feel martyred, badger their colleagues and tell them to piss off. Nobody confronts them until it's too late; then they get it in the neck and never receive either the appreciation they deserve or the constructive criticism they need.

Valery told me he was sorry he had spoken so critically about Sergei. In thinking it over, he said, he realized that, however aggravating Sergei might be, he was the only one who had the energy to really do anything for the group. "All the rest of us, well, we want things to happen and we have lots of ideas, but when it comes to doing the work, we'd rather go paint. There really is no one else. But I have no desire to go to that meeting and hear all these unpleasant things."

▲ ▲ ▲

The meeting heated up pretty quickly. Elena accused Sergei of being secretive and making decisions without consulting anyone else. "For instance, you went to Moscow at TEII expense without checking. You contracted that terrible poster without consultation. And what about the American show? You haven't told us a thing. If it weren't for Barbara we wouldn't know anything. We don't know even who the other participants are, or when the show will be, or how the money will be handled."

"And you, Barbara," someone added, "why did you call Sergei the leader of the Tovarishchestvo in your article? Did he tell you he was the leader? Do you think of him as the leader?"

I was startled. "He has the slides," I answered, "and it's Sergei who has arranged the visits to the artists, who has gone with me to these various offices, gone down to Moscow, filled out the forms. I do think of him as the leader."

"Well, what *is* the situation with the show? What about the finances?" Elena turned on Sergei, very angry, accusatory. Valentin joined in. Fingers pointed at Yul also, but mostly, at Sergei, who, standing a bit removed, leaned on a table near me. Quite quiet, looking sad and angry. "Power," Valentin had said, "it's a Russian disease. Power has gone to his head and needs to be taken from him." But I didn't hear him repeat that in the meeting.

After a while Sergei began to fight back. Angry. "Who is going to do the work if I don't do it?" He tried to explain why the Moscow poster had come out so badly but the others interrupted. "Shut up and give me a chance to talk," Sergei shouted. Arguments erupted, sub-discussions, and various people called for order. Elena was venomous; Valentin coldly angry; Tykotskii, a constant initiator of sub-conversations, would drift off telling stories, then insist that we tell him everything that had been said.

After about three hours I had had it. My eyes hurt from the smoke, I was hungry and heartsick. I caught a tram back to the hotel and took myself out to the rooftop restaurant for dinner.

▲ ▲ ▲

I know that many of these troubles have been simmering for a while, but I wonder also if their coming to a boil just now doesn't stem from the new sense of freedom. When the state was the common enemy, irritations and philosophical differences could be overlooked. It was "us against them." But now Tovarishchestvo shows are uncensored, the Wilds exhibit all over the USSR, the Group of Fourteen have proposals from Sweden and Germany, and buyers from foreign countries drift in to the artists' apartments. At the same time, ironically, attendance at the current exhibit is way down. Sergei thinks it is because the location is new and a bit hard to find, but I think that Tovarishchestvo work, no longer forbidden, has ceased to titillate the viewer. What was once shocking has become accepted truth. Perhaps from here on only serious art lovers will be interested. The bonds are loosening.

▲ ▲ ▲

The night after the meeting at Zhenya's, Sergei told me that the council decided that one out of every three council members should resign; somehow it has come to a choice between him and Yul. "I may well step aside," he said.

"He always says that," Yul told me later as we settled on a bus together going south. "This is not the first time everyone has blown up at each other. Resignation has both its appeal and its threat.

"Sergei is the motor," he went on. "With him, I can work, but he is the main one. By myself I have neither the initiative nor the energy to do it. But he can't do it without me either, even though he is the main one. I don't know what we are going to do or how this will be resolved. The others just don't do the work."

▲ ▲ ▲

I am quite apprehensive now about our invitation to Valentin, Elena and Sergei to come to America for the show. If Valentin and Elena continue to be so hateful to Sergei, suspicious and angry, having the three of them together would be a nightmare. Sergei may not be able to come anyway; aside from not being eligible for vacation time yet, he has such a reputation as troublemaker that he may not be given an exit visa, but I will go ahead and try, and hope that things either iron out or completely come to a head.

2 2 . F I N A L I N S T R U C T I O N S

My last night, racing to touch all bases. At three o'clock I went to my old friends, Maria and Marina's, to say goodbye and of course to eat and to receive presents. I had forgotten the inevitability of presents and, having already stuffed one suitcase full of Timur, Africa and Kotelnikov's hangings, my drawings, art equipment, tapes, film, cutting boards and records, without even starting to pack my clothes, I groaned audibly, I'm afraid, when Maria handed me a teapot, a vase for a friend, dishtowels and a lamp for my daughter Robin, and started combing the shelves for books for my granddaughter. "Explain to your mother," I pleaded desperately to Marina, close to tears. "Explain that I already have more than I can carry. I have two boxes of paintings as well as my suitcases. They charge huge amounts if you have extra things." But Maria herself was close to tears and Marina, never having flown, had no idea what I was talking about. "But Barbara," she said, "she wants you to have nice presents so you'll remember us." So I tried to hide my panic and be grateful for having friends.

I returned to the hotel just in time to receive the call from Zhenya Orlov. "We're downstairs with the paintings." He, Zhenya Tykotsky, and Valentin waited in the lobby in their knitted caps with a long roll of Elena's paintings, a cardboard sandwich of Zhenya Orlov's and Nikitina's work, and a wooden box painted green, blue and fuchsia, filled with paintings. "This box will be the new style in San Francisco," said Zhenya Orlov. "Everybody will want one." They assured me everything would be easy to dis- and reassemble for Customs.

I went down to the lobby at six to meet Gennady who had zipped in to give me his biographical data for the catalog, and got back to the room just as Yul called to say he was waiting on the corner. I grabbed my coat and ran down. The street was swarming with militia and plainclothes men. Yul was nowhere in sight and for a minute I was afraid he had been picked up—a closed van, the sort they put people in, waited at the corner—but he came walking towards me motioning to go down the steps into the Metro. Even there he wouldn't speak, though we walked arm in arm, and wouldn't talk till we got into a phone booth. There he gave me the tape he had made, at my request, about his life. It is supposed to be his statement for the catalog, but Yul is incapable of being brief or of sticking to the topic of art. Much of the tape is undoubtedly political and could be dangerous to him if intercepted.

Back in the hotel again I gathered myself together for the evening: a bag for Sergei and Alyona of leftover film, tapes, post-its, undelivered presents such as calendars, a Paul Winter tape, socks, and lists of things yet to resolve. I had resisted as many commissions from U.S. friends as I could—please call this psychologist in Vilnius, mail a sweater to my sister in Vladivostok, deliver some urgent photographs to the Ministry of Culture in Moscow, tell Andrei I still love him and ask why hasn't he written—but had saddled myself with a few which I was now leaving to Sergei.

Alyona and I took the bus out to the university where Sergei now works "full-time" as furnace-stoker, on for twenty-four hours, then off for three days. Yul works fewer hours at his furnaces, and earns less, but is still considered full-time. His conditions are worse, he says—very noisy and always damp—but still not involving such heavy labor as Oleg Kotelnikov's over the coal burners. The drawback to Sergei's new job is that he is not allowed to take off for an hour as he could before; he must be there with only short breaks for meals. Yet there is nothing to do but be present to shut off the valves in case of emergency. Except to bail. A three-foot hole in the concrete floor in the back room fills with water from a leak in the boiler. If he doesn't keep up with it the basement floods. So every couple of hours he bails with a bucket into a large standing bin, whence the water recirculates slowly back to the floor.

The basement itself is dry and reasonably warm. Sergei has a cubicle off the furnace-room with a bed, table and chair, and a black and white TV. In the furnace-room is a larger, well-lit table where he can write or draw. He comes equipped with things to do. The furnaces themselves are quite gorgeously yellow and blue—a row of clean, colorful monsters shumming away.

We sat in Sergei's cubbyhole eating the meat pie Alyona had brought, and went over our lists: finances to date; what I had paid for what works; list of titles; full names of artists; statements for the catalog still needed; distribution of the slides taken in November—Sergei didn't want to give them to the artists because the quality was poor, but I said we had promised and must honor that promise—and, finally, how we are to communicate from now on. We agreed on a once-a-month call during the last three days of each month; he'll leave the phone plugged in those nights.

"My phone is still bugged," he said, "'glasnost' or no 'glasnost,' so be careful what you say. Don't talk about money and don't mention last names, just to be safe. You shouldn't be talking about money with the artists either, actually, they just gossip and spread rumors and compete with each other. The less information they have the better."

Alyona was coming down with a sore throat and was curled up on the bed, my scarf wrapped around her neck. Around eleven Sergei walked us to the bus. It was a cold sparkling night; St. Isaac's loomed across the river, backlit by the city streets. The river flowed gray and soft. A silt of snow had sifted seductively onto the ice underfoot. We walked holding each other trying not to fall. A hurried hug and a kiss as the bus came, then sobs with Alyona as we left Sergei on the curb. She walked me to the hotel door and we said goodbye.

PART V

May

1988

23. OVER CALIFORNIA WINE

*I*t's five a.m., a full moon. I'm wide awake. Valentin, too, is awake—I can see the light under his door. He and Elena have been at my home in Berkeley for a week. Valentin is in my study, Elena in the bedroom, and I am camping out in the living room. I am relieved they got here in time, given all the last minute ticket and visa snags, but they touched down safely, tired and replete with newly purchased Marlboros. They like it here. People are helpful. Americans understand their English, things are beautiful, clean. You can buy good cigarettes.

We have been all over Berkeley, San Francisco and out to the gallery in Point Reyes where the show is already hung, and sit till late hours drinking tea or wine in the kitchen. Valentin wakes early and has taken to fixing me breakfast; Elena wakes late and slowly. In the car, she sits beside me controlling the tape deck—she rejects all music except Ella Fitzgerald—and dreams out the window. Valentin asks about everything. It is exactly the difference in their art work: Valentin observant to the most intimate detail, even incorporating real found items, and Elena reaching deep inside herself for images to express feelings and ideas.

They have questions about everything, especially how much people earn and what things cost. On the street they drop into every open door, finger the sweatshirts, the key chains, the running shoes. They have already bought cameras and shoes. Elena pulled us into a leather shop and tried on a full-length white fox coat. "It's not becoming to me," she decided surveying herself in the mirror, "Maybe they have something in another color?" To my relief, they didn't.

While I have been loving getting to know Valentin and Elena, it has been painful to me that Sergei could not be here to represent the Tovarishchestvo. We invited Elena as the strongest woman artist, and Valentin, because—next to Yul, who claims he will never be given an exit visa—he has been the most helpful to me. Elena and Valentin have both been in the leadership of the Tovarishchestvo since its beginning, they are respected by the other artists and have caught on how to talk to me in basic Russian, but Sergei as my main colleague is the one who really should be at the opening.

Even in December I had been getting mixed messages from him about our invitation. He would say he was eager to come, but then, for instance, I heard from Alyona that they were applying to go to Bulgaria in May, the very time of the show.

"Do you really want to come to Point Reyes?" I asked him one day. "Are you serious about this? It's not worth it to me to go through all these grant applications if you are not."

"How can you ask? Of course I want to." But later he said, "Well, but I have this new job, and I have only had it for two

months. I probably won't get any vacation for six months."
Should I wait, I asked him, and invite him for next December
when the show moves to San Francisco? "Oh," he said airily, "I'll
come in both May and December." Then in March he phoned to
say that, once and for all, his boss refused to sign the permit for
him to take off from work, so he could not come.

The friction between Valentin and Elena on the one side and
Sergei and Yul on the other has if anything intensified. It has
come to the point where, when Valentin went to greet him at a
recent meeting, Yul replied coolly, "How are you, Valentin
Ivanovich?" Such formal address to a former intimate is a real
slap in the face.

Generally Valentin, Elena and I stay clear of these matters,
but they crop up. At the gallery the other night I suggested a
group photo and moved everyone over in front of Yul's triptych.
"No," protested Elena, brows stormy, "we won't have our picture taken in front of that painting." And she made us move
around the corner.

▲ ▲ ▲

A couple of nights ago we invited a group of artists, some
people from my Russophile community, and random friends to
my studio to see Elena's slides of Leningrad women artists. The
studio is down in a seedy section of Berkeley where the home-
less find shelter and sometimes pick up work in small manufac-
turing plants. Daytimes it smells of chemicals from the local tan-
nery. Our camouflage-green corrugated steel building houses a
glass-making outfit, a photographer and me. Elena and Valentin
ruthlessly cleaned up my space and hung up pieces of art by each
of us. My landlord, the glassmaker, carried in large benches from
the yard and we set out wine and juice on the work tables.

I was astonished at the variety of artists whose slides Elena
had brought: a series of paintings by the blockade artist, Lenina
Nikitina, about the women she encountered during her stay in a
mental hospital; some decorative pieces about turn-of-the-cen-
tury fashions; nostalgic primitively painted village scenes; wild

new paintings by Elena Shevelenko/Marta Volkova; and some disturbing self-portraits Elena herself had done four or five years ago. This is just the tip of the iceberg, she told us, there are many more excellent artists trying to surface.

Having heard Elena light in to the Tovarishchestvo about the difficulties women encounter I had assumed we would be in for a rousing feminist evening, but Elena led off by saying firmly and unequivocally that there was absolutely no difference between women and men artists. She parried all attempts to probe further. Knowing how difficult it was for her to speak in public, I didn't challenge her and, while some of the audience expressed doubts, Elena was unbudgeable, turning often to Valentin for support.

I had warned Valentin not to take over. I have been trying to curb him a bit at public meetings. He answers all questions and, if Elena breaks in, he is back again as soon as she takes a breath. He has so much he wants to say it is hard to keep quiet. "You go into things in too much detail," Elena told him, so "detail" has become the watchword.

Elena later agreed that she had stopped any penetrating talk about women's issues in the beginning. But why? She shrugged. Something between her and Valentin, perhaps. Or maybe she simply became shy in front of so many strangers, or reluctant to hang out the Tovarishchestvo's dirty laundry in public.

We came home quite late and uncorked a bottle of wine. "So many people asked me why I paint what I paint," Elena complained, settling in at the kitchen table. "How am I supposed to answer that question? How do *I* know why I do what I do? I don't have anything to say, let them just look at the work. Doesn't it speak for itself?"

"But why do you paint cows and fish?" I asked her. "You are not a country dweller."

"I don't know," she answered. She looked at me balefully and swirled the wine in her glass. Her straight blond hair fell over the right side of her face. "Maybe some of it is nostalgia for a simpler life. I spent my first years in the country and still go there whenever I can. I like to fish, to just get off by myself. And cows, well, cows are just like people. You can feel their sadness and their pain. It's difficult for everyone, this business of living." She paused a minute and looked uncomfortable at having gotten so serious. I was afraid she would stop.

"I think I'm really dealing with issues of good and evil," she went on. "I want to know, honestly, what is the proportion of good in human beings and what's the proportion of evil. How much more good is there than evil? To what extent are people more beautiful than ugly, or more ugly than beautiful? Since I do not know that, I cannot say whether people by nature are good or evil. Why is it that a person may *not* be beautiful on the outside, but be beautiful on the inside? I am exploring such things." She paused and smiled. "So far I haven't established anything." She rocked her glass on the table.

"Now I've said too much. I'm going to be really embarrassed if you print any of that in your book."

"I probably will," I said, looking at her over my glasses.

"Oh, God, I hate to think of it." Elena brushed back her hair. "Why don't we talk about *your* work for a while?" and she grinned and refilled my glass.

24. POINT REYES WELCOMES LENINGRAD

Point Reyes is at its best in May, the grass still lush from late spring rains and the fields a pointillist carpet of lupine, butter-and-eggs, wild iris, lacy cream and pink mustard. Cow parsnip blossoms crawl from their green pods. Turkey vultures sail speculatively overhead and red-wing blackbirds sing arias in the reeds.

The community of Point Reyes Station lies among dairy, cattle and horse ranches in rolling hills which turn bright green in winter and golden brown in summer. A thickly forested ridge rises between the ocean and long narrow Tomales Bay. Along the ocean stretch miles of spectacular beaches. Many of the houses were built at the turn of the century when Point Reyes Station was a busy port that sent lumber and fish products by rail to San Francisco. The trains have long since ceased to run. Residents today come from varied ethnic backgrounds and lifestyles: farmers and ranchers, retired people, artists, recently arrived Mexican Americans, and a very few remaining Native Americans. Urbanites from the San Francisco Bay area have weekend houses here or drive out for the day to hike and dine in the many fine restaurants.

Valentin, Elena and I have been staying in a home loaned by some generous strangers. I get up early and walk to Mike's Cafe for coffee. The mornings are cool and sparkling. Cows mill on the levee. The whine of the garbage truck comes in and out of focus as it cruises the quiet streets. Mike's is full, noisy and steamy, smelling of bacon and work-clothes. I drink my coffee, a stranger at the counter, and return to the slumbering house.

▲ ▲ ▲

The opening reception had drawn a crowd larger than the gallery has seen for several years. People came from all over the Bay Area—those who had heard about the show from the media or were friends of gallery members, or friends of Valentin and Elena's from the Russian emigre community, or those simply curious about the USSR. The passage outside the gallery throbbed with Russian and English.

Midafternoon I called everyone together in the main room, Russian style. In America we usually do not give speeches at receptions but so many had come from so far it seemed appropriate to have a ceremony of some sort. I explained briefly how the show had come about, and introduced Valentin and Elena. Only veiled threats from me persuaded them to come in to speak, for they had been escaping the crowd as often as possible, smoking in the passageway with their emigree acquaintances. Elena, Valentin and I climbed up on the platform we had rigged up from a sculpture stand. Valentin spoke through a translator. "This is the first show our unofficial artists have had beyond our country's borders," he said. "We are grateful for the chance to show you our work, and hope it is just the beginning of a long relationship between the artists of Leningrad and San Francisco. Perhaps in this way we can come to understand each other better and bring some of this to our politicians."

Elena as usual was briefer. She greeted the crowd in English. "Thank you for everything," she said blushing, and then, grabbing my hand and Valentin's, she raised them high in the air. "We did it!" she cried. "We did it!"

▲ ▲ ▲

I feel very proud about this show. We worked so hard, climbed so many stairs, filled out so many forms, and here the result—forty-five pieces by twenty-one artists—glows on the walls in Point Reyes, much as it had glowed on the walls over a year ago in Tsovik's Easter studio. The tone of the work is much darker than our usual California show: surfaces are crowded, the humor ironic rather than playful, and the subjects are of hope maintained through tragedy and loss, but it looks good. It encompasses everything from Sergei's dark abstractions to Zhenya Orlov's decorative villages, Tykotskii's Jewish wanderers, Nikitina's blockade victims, Zhilina's cat by the fishbowl, and Afonichev's orange and black Roman bloodbaths. Valentin's jewel-like paintings of the city and of Gregory Soroka are by the entrance to the gallery; ahead is Yul's philosophical triptych pondering the fate of the earth, and around the corner across the room Elena's vibrant colors dominate.

While it is a small show in a small town, for most people here it is the first direct contact with anyone or anything from the Soviet Union. It was moving to see so many come to the opening. I had actually been afraid there might be incidents of name calling, spray painting, vandalism, whatever—so many years of evil-empire rhetoric cannot be quickly undone—but the feeling of the day was celebratory. Point Reyes truly welcomed the Leningrad artists.

Much of the work sold immediately: two Tykotsky's, one of Lenina Nikitina's, both of Valentin's and of Elena's, and Sasha Gurevich's rainbow. A Zubkov and a Mikhailov. The gallery log filled with, "Wonderful! Amazing to see such variety! Thanks for letting us see into your hearts! Such competence and vision! A most moving exhibit!" I, of course, am thrilled by this; Elena and Valentin are not so thrilled.

"Grrreat!" they say sarcastically, "vonderrrfool! marrrvelous! peace and friendship! But what do people really think about our work? There is not one word of criticism in this book. No one wants to know why we do this or that, or what so-and-so means by his images. How does our work look to American artists? Are we just curiosities or are we real artists? Who is going to talk to us about that?"

"I have so much wanted to meet and talk with American artists," Valentin said. "I want to talk about what we are drawing and how we put paints on canvas, what themes we choose, and in general about everything, everything that concerns artists. Is it a problem with language or are Americans just too polite?"

Perhaps we are too polite, at least in public, although I have participated in some brutal sessions in artists' studios. I heard somewhere that Americans expect each other to lie in public and to tell the truth in private, whereas Russians expect the opposite. That's hard to believe since in the Soviet Union the public lie is practically an art form, but I was reminded by Valentin's remark of the intensity of interactions at my very first Tovarishchestvo show in the fall of 1984, with all the artists arguing and gesticulating, soaking up criticism, basking in praise or hunkering to the defence. We Americans do tend to be less confrontative.

▲ ▲ ▲

After the opening Elena, Valentin and I sat in the kitchen of our borrowed house. The evening cooled at sunset and the town quieted as weekenders headed home. A light breeze slapped bushes against the siding. We shared a sense of unreality: are they, Valentin and Elena, Leningraders, really here with me in

America? Are we really drinking chilled chardonnay together in a country house with sliding doors to a patio overlooking an inlet to the Pacific? Did we really, together with so many others, put on a show of Leningrad work in America?

Once again, I missed Sergei. It is he who best articulates dreams for the Tovarishchestvo and the hopes that a show in the United States may help legitimate the status of the unofficial artists. And it is he, in truth, who was my guide into this complex and dark world. I missed his gloomy presence and his guidance for the future.

▲ ▲ ▲

We sipped our wine quietly. A symphony of bug and frog song slipped under the doors. A cricket sawed away on the hearth. During the afternoon a critic from one of the art journals, come to see the show, had been overheard to say, "Nothing new. It's all very derivative." Just as my prospective emigrant acquaintance Igor had predicted. But didn't the critic miss the point?

In the redwood forests shadowing the road to Point Reyes you may stand in the centers of innumerable overlapping circles of second growth redwoods. The parent trees which have been cut down, struck by lightning or simply rotted with age, open up space for the saplings which rise from their roots, slim and graceful, circling the husk of the parent. Nourishment is drawn from the old as the new generation fills the forest and the sky. Are the new trees derivative? Are they innovative? Are they beautiful?

E P I L O G U E

*T*he confusion and upheavals we read about in the news have had consequences in the lives of my friends—after six years of perestroika most of my friends simply feel anxious.

Life has changed radically for the artists since the 1987 January show when they were first permitted to sell work to the public. Starting in 1988, after Soviet paintings sold for stupendous prices at a Sotheby auction in Moscow, Soviet artists were besieged by requests to show in the West. Unofficial artists were more in demand than the formerly compliant members of the

Artists Union. Every dealer who could afford a translator wanted to be the first to show contemporary work from behind the Iron Curtain and hoped to bag a new "Chagall" or "Malevich." The newly franchised Soviet cooperatives, too, looked to make a killing exporting paintings or publishing catalogs. In addition, art had become one of the few forms of convertible currency Soviet citizens travelling or emigrating to the West might carry with them.

Dealers discovered Leningrad only after Moscow had been gleaned, but, by the summer of 1989, conversation in Leningrad studios might swing between comparing notes on how to get tickets to London or New York, arguing the merits of such-and-such a dealer's offer, and trying to decide whether it would be more prestigious to show in San Diego or in Boston—topics unthinkable even two years earlier.

Sergei's hope that Leningrad unofficial art could emerge into the light of the world had come true. The artists could finally work for an audience larger than each other. The Gallery Route One exhibit we had worked so hard for was only a precursor to solo and group shows in Dusseldorf and Paris, in Stockholm and London. Excellent shows featuring the unofficial Leningrad artists have been held in Los Angeles, Seattle and Columbus and travelling exhibitions—including ours—tour the country. Timur and Afrika and others of the New Artists have become denizens of New York where they come to show and often work for months. Zhenya Orlov slips in and out of Sweden. One of Slava Afonichev's paintings sold at auction in London for an elegant price. Lenina Nikitina's blockade series has shown in Germany, and Valentin and Elena travel to Hamburg and Berlin as well as to see me in Berkeley.

▲ ▲ ▲

The cultural scene in Leningrad, too, has opened up. In January 1989, the Leningrad Artists Union, at that time still a viable organization, opened a joint exhibit with the Tovarishchestvo in the Central Exhibition Hall, the most prestigious hall in town.

The union work, appropriately enough, hung on the right and the TEII work, including pieces by artists long dead or emigrated—Arefeyev, Chemyakin, Rukhin—hung on the left. "We will see," mused Sergei, "which is considered more truly to be art." Predictably, viewers at the show crowded to the left and gave the official work only a cursory run-through.

Russian museums, meanwhile, have been borrowing back the works of Malevich, of Kandinsky, of Pavel Filonov from sources throughout the world, and mounting blockbuster shows in Moscow and Leningrad. Exchanges have begun with many of the major museums of the world.

The fact that contemporary Leningrad art is being taken seriously in the West has led even the Russian authorities to take another look at work only a few years ago considered little better than graffiti. The Russian Museum has been buying pieces by the unofficial artists, including work by Elena and Valentin, and curators from other Russian museums cruise the larger shows to make purchases. This change in attitude creeps slowly, however, paralyzed both by out-of-date curatorial sensibilities and by lack of funds, while, unfortunately, much of the finest work is syphoned off to the West.

▲ ▲ ▲

One of the best things that has happened to many of the artists is the acquisition of studio space. In the spring of 1989, word got around that a building near the center of town, just off Nevsky Prospekt, would rent to artists. By mid-summer the building, condemned and awaiting major renovation, had become the de facto center for the unofficial artists. Off the courtyard Elena, Valentin, Yul and Sergei, and seventy or more old-guard unofficials and new young artists have taken studio space. Two galleries of erratic quality and schedule, several rock bands and theater groups, a number of international trade organizations and various shady characters have all moved in.

Elena has given me a key to her three-room studio, and use of the small back room. Valentin gives me drawing paper that he gets in trade with a mortician—they line caskets with it—and I use Elena's paints if mine run out. Sergei brings me sausages and cheese.

I come up from the depths of the metro into the very heart of the city. Buses, trolleys and trams circle in front of the Moscow Station and head off in one of five directions. I cross Nevsky Prospekt in a surge of pedestrians, lope along past crowded coffee and tea shops—where little tea and no coffee can be had—past stand-up cafeterias and outdoor mineral water stands, and turn into Pushkinskaya Street. It is suddenly quiet. The street is lined with five- and six-story buildings. A scientific bookstore attracts few customers with its display of dusty paperbacks. A power saw shrills briefly from a storefront being remodeled.

Number Ten Pushkinskaya is one of those square nineteenth century five-story apartment houses entered from a central courtyard. Dust and trash overflow the bins in the yard, and old doors, broken window frames and glass litter the halls. The archway and entry halls smell of urine. Cars shudder in and out over potholes and rock music vibrates the airshafts.

No one has swept for a long time. None of the elevators work anymore—sabotaged, it was thought, by remaining residents who were resentful about the influx of long-haired artists. We keep the doors to the studio locked for there have been two murders in the building, both black-market related, and not infrequent robberies and beatings, especially of people who have travelled to the West. We have also been hearing of an art mafia dealing in stolen paintings.

Elena was one of the first to begin to work here in the spring of 1989. She found two sofas and some hard chairs, and a hot plate to make tea and to cook up sizing for her canvases. The walls are covered with paintings she is assembling for a show in Pennsylvania. The table, and the floor under the table, is piled with drawings, photographs, contracts, catalogs and overflowing ashtrays.

Valentin, whose studio is off a neighboring stairwell, has set up his printmaking operation. His doorbell rings constantly. He lets in a stream of artists, dealers, and Soviet middlemen. Because

Valentin has one of the few phones in the building, other residents drop in to make calls or get messages and stay for tea.

Not that it's any different at Elena's. In a typical week we let through the door a man who wants to discuss final details on an upcoming catalog, a photographer to take or deliver photos, a curator from a Dutch museum, a gallery director from Paris, a group of Americans or Germans, friends of friends, and the whole matrix of artists from the Tovarishchestvo.

▲ ▲ ▲

The artists have all become a little crazy. Some of them have been beseiged with requests to show; the rest would like to be. Pressure to produce mounts as the artists accept every possible offer. The new studios make it possible at last to paint large paintings, to make messes, to work long hours. Some thrive under the new freedoms and deepen their explorations; some suffer the paralysis that can follow a dropping of restrictions, or flail in all directions. Some simply copy their own earlier work. Most doubt the permanence of change and have been hustling to take advantage of the opening while it lasts—to paint, to publish, to travel, to make some money, to find their identities as artists in the world art market.

New questions arise: What is a painting worth? How does a dollar relate to a ruble? Can I lower my price if a piece doesn't sell? Or raise it if a tourist wants it very much? More troubling questions: Can I turn out enough for a show? For two shows? What if I run out of ideas? What if I run out of paint? Maybe I should horde a bit to be sure? Should I take this dealer to see my friend or keep the contact to myself?

Questions arise, also, about what to paint. For many years, the only way to tell the truth about daily life in the Soviet Union was through the arts. Those writers, musicians and artists who dared to express, usually in metaphor, what no one could say aloud became cultural heroes. Everyone knew the words of songs by the irreverent Vysotsky and Galich although few were ever published by Melodia, the official music publisher. When 50,000 people waited in the shattering cold to see the Tovarishchestvo show in January 1987, it was because the artists were expressing feelings seldom articulated, perhaps for many people not yet even conscious. Art has not been so crucial in America where anyone can tell the truth and not be punished for it. Usually. Now what should they paint about?

"I think my work is getting worse," Elena said one morning. She had been wrestling with the color of a face, now darker, now redder. "Tell me what you think, honestly. Was it better before?"

"I liked it better," I said. "The faces were somehow deeper. These are getting awfully anonymous."

"I know," she said sadly, "I think I'm getting worse. And it's the most important thing in the world to me to paint better all the time. I can't even get the color right anymore. I like something okay, and then I try to fix it up to be just right and I spoil it." She stubbed out her cigarette. "Lots of people like my work so much, but I'm afraid it's because it's gotten pretty. Look at those colors. Sweet, sweet; it's disgusting! Phoo!

"I don't know," she went on after a minute. "I can't seem to pull out of this. I have the feeling something new is coming but I can't go back to the old and I can't get out of this stage yet. I need to stretch some new canvases. Maybe once things settle down a bit I can get on with something."

But things are not settling down. The art market has gone bust and the Russian fad has peaked. Money is tight, unemployment rising, and prices skyrocketing. Tea, meat, cheese, macaroni, soap and sugar had all been rationed for a year or more, but now restrictions are off and you can buy anything, assuming you can both find and afford it. One of my 80-year-old grandma friends hunted all day for meat at any price and came home empty-handed. Matches simply aren't to be found anywhere. Tomorrow they will appear and socks will disappear. Of course there is no coffee. The small supply of soap will hardly do the dishes and serve for bathing, to say nothing of washing clothes. Beer is impossible to find, cheese is only an occasional item, onions come already bagged and five out of six are sprouting. Carrots and tomatoes can only be found in the "free market," the *rynok,* at high prices. Life is really tough for people with no money and no country sources of food—family members from a village or with dachas, or relatives in Georgia.

Supplies are short not only of food and clothing but of paint, drawing paper, canvas, stretcher bars, glue. All these necessities of the trade are hard to come by, even for those with access to union stores. Rumors of worse to come keep everyone on edge.

The daily frustrations and uncertainties of life in Russia underlie the increasing rates of crime and violence; indeed many of my friends' lives here seem filled with trauma and tragedy. Some doctor friends, whose salaries the hospital can no longer pay, are selling off their books to pay for food. Zhenya Orlov has spent days dealing with the aftermath of a robbery in his apartment and with threats against his teenage son. Another friend's wife is in the last stages of alcoholism; yet another artist's ex-wife comes sobbing to his studio over her lonely life. A friend of Sergei's was beaten within an inch of death by some thugs, reputedly hired by his wife. "They hit him here on the bridge of the nose," said Sergei demonstrating. "It would have been a death-blow but they missed by just a bit. People can't even talk to each other anymore, they just want to hit something. Anybody can hire these thugs—just give them a little money and they'll beat up anyone you want."

I commented to Elena on the amount of drinking going on among our friends.

"Life is just as frustrating as it ever was," she said. "By the time people here reach a certain age, say thirty or thirty-five, they lose interest in living. Then if they are to go on, they either get terribly interested in money or they drink. Most of *our* friends drink. For some, it's just occasional bouts, like at parties. But for others it's chronic. It's the system. Everything one tries to do is frustrated. Even though, theoretically, we're moving towards capitalism, if you actually try to raise your head a bit above the crowd you get shot down as an 'egoist,' a 'businessman.' When the artists get together no one can agree on anything anymore. Everybody's suspicious and pursuing his own advantage."

▲ ▲ ▲

People are looking for reasons why things are so bad here. Some blame the covert grip of the old communists, saying that they intentionally sabotage production and distribution in order to create dissatisfaction with the free market. Others say that entrepreneurs have bought up all desirable goods to hoard and then resell at a profit. Hopes that Yeltsin could move faster than Gorbachev towards democracy and prosperity are foundering on the depressing realities of lay-offs and shortages.

Since everything is available for a price on the black market and since some dealers are thus getting conspicuously rich, and since some of these dealers are Jews, it's only a step to blame the Jews for shortages. Anti-Semitism is becoming quite blatant. I have heard that part of the initiation fee to the nationalistic organization, Pamyat, is a list of three new names and addresses of Jews. Swastikas are on the walls everywhere; someone drew them on Zhenya Tykotskii's paintings when he had a show at Moscow State University.

"You can feel a new wave of anti-Semitism gathering," a Jewish friend said to me. "Everyone is ready to beat up on someone, they are so frustrated. All this talk, and things are just getting worse and worse." Many of the Jews I know are trying to emigrate.

"Do you think it is in our blood, somehow," Slava Afonichev asked one day, "that we can't cooperate with each other? We just don't know how to work collegially—all we can think to do is to try to be the boss, to dominate."

"What does America think of all this?" people ask me.

I answer, "America believes that everything has changed here. They say, 'How exciting it must be now in Russia with all the changes!'"

My Russian friends shake their heads despondently.

Yul has warned me not to be naive. "All these so-called new freedoms are being 'given' to us, Barbara. That's great, it's exciting, but they could just as easily take them all back if the mood strikes them. Nothing is written into law yet. We have no rights."

▲ ▲ ▲

Although all the artists who exhibit in the West proudly list their long affiliation with the Tovarishchestvo, just at the moment when their dreams for legitimization might be realized, the association has become largely irrelevent. Back when time and space were so tight, and style and content of art so restricted, the independent artists fought hard to retain their integrity and to support each other. They shared a history and a struggle. But, as the Communist Party lost its power and the Artists Union's benefits have begun to erode, the Tovarishchestvo's unity as an "out" group dissolved. The more successful TEII artists have been pulled to show in the West. A few, like Yulia Ivanova, slipped away to join the union. The New Artists (formerly the Wilds) operate completely on their own.

The old guard of the Tovarishchestvo continue to nurse grudges from the bitterness of events surrounding that painful January meeting I attended. All the then members of the council—Yul, Sergei, Valentin, Elena, Zhenya Orlov, Tykotskii, all— were thrown out that spring. They were replaced by a younger crew who had little patience for the work involved. Since pulling off the big Central Exhibition Hall show with the Artists Union, where everyone came together one more time for a sweet moment of vindication, the Tovarishchestvo has done practically nothing. A few of the old members including Gennady Zubkov have been trying to build a new artist's organization, this time with sanction from Moscow, but the general response from the artists has been, "Who needs it?" The Tovarishchestvo leadership is burned out.

▲ ▲ ▲

The fate of the artists' studios at #10 Pushkinskaya remains uncertain. Originally the city administration gave the building to a cooperative whose job was to see that the toilets and door knobs weren't stolen while the building waited empty for renovation. The cooperative, The Guardians, put Sergei in charge of distributing studio space. Sergei and Yul, however, saw the possibility to realize their dream of a cultural center. This center could provide not only studio space for qualified artists but facilities for printmaking, film editing, ceramics and an archive documenting the independent art movement. They formed a foundation, the Humanities Fund for Free Culture.

Yul—who meanwhile had been elected to the city council and now sat on some key committees—petitioned the city for jurisdiction over the building, and received it. The Guardians were understandably not pleased—revenues from the various co-ops and international businesses with offices in the building are substantial. The Guardians have refused to cede management, continue to collect rents, and have brought suit against the foundation. Sergei and Yul had the phone company cut off their telephones. Leningrad's mayor, Anatoly Sobchak, occasionally loses patience with the whole business and threatens repossession by the city; the city bureaucracy, unsettled by all this wrangling, periodically shuts off the water or the electricity and threatens to turn everyone out.

The Fund's jurisdiction over the building comes with strings attached. They must undertake renovation of the building themselves, immediately. It is uncertain where the money to do this is to come from, although Sergei hints enigmatically at foreign investors. Even if the Fund manages to finance the renovation, the city has retained the right to receive rents from two-thirds of the remodeled building. This leaves little space for Yul and Sergei's grand plans and for studios for the artists. In spite of all this, the Fund is moving ahead: with money from a small grant by San Francisco's Tides Foundation, they have ordered detailed architectural drawings and begun a radical overhaul of the ancient drains.

These jurisdictional shennanigans exasperate the artist-tenants who don't know from one month to the next whether to brace for eviction. They don't want to get drawn into taking sides. "The hell with them all," is the general attitude, "just let us paint and get on with it."

"Endless 'ifs' have impregnated the air the whole country breathes," Sergei told me when we were talking about the building. "No one is sure of tomorrow. We have studios now, it's true, and if in the near future our foundation does not go bankrupt, or if the whole independent movement does not go bust, or isn't abolished by the authorities, then perhaps, perhaps, it will be easier for us to work."

▲ ▲ ▲

Alyona and Sergei had come to California at long last in the spring of 1989, but it was not a happy visit. Sergei brought with him all the worries and workaholism that plague him at home, without the flexibility or connections that enable him to accomplish so much in Leningrad. He arrived with three large agendas: to set up TEII shows in American galleries; to paint some large new pieces in my studio; and to film his stay in America. He had little success in any but the last. Tensions flared, he and Alyona fought, and by the time we all returned to Leningrad in May their relationship was in serious trouble. And Alyona was pregnant with their son, Fedya. Sergei subsequently moved to his studio in the Pushkinskaya building, where he receives an endless stream of visitors and supplicants. After Fedya was born, Alyona moved with him to a larger apartment on the south side of town, and their old apartment became mine in an exchange too Byzantine to relate.

Sergei and Alyona are not the only ones whose personal lives have undergone changes. Yul and Natasha broke up. Yul has a new young wife and baby daughter, and has served two years on the Leningrad City Council. He told the full story of his past as dissident activist in an interview in one of Leningrad's major papers. Yul's phone in the Pushkinskaya Street building rings constantly with requests from constituents. He appears in the artists' studios wearing a three-piece suit and a tired look, and shakes his head with the futility of it all, but he is happy in a way I have not seen him before. Only he never has time to paint.

Valentin has left his marriage also. He and Elena have bought a car together. Valentin drives each morning from his apartment on the north side to the far south to pick her up. They do errands together. Valentin cooks dinner in his studio in the evening for

Elena, Pasha—Valentin's son, the one who asked me so long ago about Madonna and Michael Jackson—and for me when I am in town.

Elena still lives at home with her parents and her sister, although she has bought a fine apartment not far from Valentin's. Her mother would be devastated without her, she says. She and Valentin are designing a dacha somewhere not far from the Finnish border, where the two of them and Elena's mother can get out of the city, sunbathe and fish.

Rising anti-Semitism led Marta Volkova and Slava Shevelenko to emigrate to Holland in 1991. They had previously taken 10-year-old Anya out of school and had been tutoring her and young Vasya at home. "Anya's so bright and lively," Marta had told me, "but she has been threatened at school for being Jewish. Every year as the school year goes on she becomes depressed and secretive. It takes us most of the summer to get her back to her real self." Slava and Marta's paintings have sold well in the West; their prospects are good.

Some of the artists continue to work at home, even though studios are now available to them. Zhenya Orlov, in whose living-room we had so many of our meetings, is repelled by the dirt, the constant interruptions, the atmosphere of dissention on Pushkinskaya. He paints quietly and consistently at home. His connection with a fine Stockholm gallery allows him to sell almost any work he does.

Lenina Nikitina also works, as before, in her small apartment with her cats and tiny dog. A beautiful half-hour film has been made of her life, her memories of the Blockade, her thoughts about religion and her art, but distribution has hit snags and, so far, it is almost impossible to buy it. Nikitina's paintings have been shown in Germany and America, and some have sold to museums. But she has not travelled. She works slowly, deliberately; it is hard for her to part with her intensely personal images, and she does not sell her work easily.

A heart attack claimed Volodya Mikhailov at the age of fifty-two. His studio had been the first I had visited back in 1986, but we had seen little of each other until the summer of 1991. At that time I went with Sergei to take him some paintings by various of the Tovarishchestvo artists, including one of my own. Volodya had worked out a possible exchange with a German surgeon, an art lover: paintings for heart surgery. Volodya was pale and breathing hard. The trip on the tram and up the stairs to the studio exhausted him. The surgeon was to come to Leningrad within the week. But the trip was postponed, and postponed again, and Volodya died early one morning in October.

▲ ▲ ▲

The night before I left for home last summer, Alyona was waiting for me at the Anichkov Bridge by the horses. She pulled me down the steps to the water where we were handed into a small motorboat. The driver swung away from the wharf. It was a bit after 11 o'clock, slightly overcast, the sky a diffused orange and gray. To me, the city of Leningrad has always been yellow; this evening the different shades of the buildings—ochre, beige, pumpkin, sand—picked up the grays and golds from the sky, and reflected them in the still canals before us, in the shattering wake behind. We skirted a cathedral on the left domed in intense cobalt, on the right a deep dusty green palace half hidden by the sycamores lining the street. All through the city people were still out, carrying packages home, strolling with friends; lovers leaned over the bridge railings or sat on the parapets. Each of the bridges over the canals has a different pattern of wrought iron railing and often sculptures stand on the corners.

We drove out into the Neva, the vista suddenly wide and gray, the city dwarfed by the width of the river. Aside from a few motorboats like ours, the great Neva was empty. Freighters can't come through until the bridges raise at two and only the very rich and enterprising have pleasure boats. It was late, of course, close to midnight, but the harbor in New York or San Francisco would have been busy.

Alyona was tired. This boat trip was, I knew, an effort for her and done only because she loves me. I had been after her since mid-June to leave Fedya with her mother and walk the city with me late at night. The peak of the White Nights had passed without us celebrating them. Nobody wants to play anymore, I complained. All the concert-going, movies, dance and jazz festivals, the long walks by the river—a thing of the past. Valentin and Elena kept asking what I'd like to do but, even though I suggested things, nothing came of it. They were working too hard.

But it's more than that. My honeymoon with Leningrad is over. It seems like a lifetime ago I had all those wonderful adventures and felt so delighted and enthusiastic about being here. Several times I have actually thought of going home to Berkeley earlier than I had planned, but even though everybody is preoccupied and at each other's throats, I am fascinated by watching these changes play out.

In detached moments, I see all this tension and turmoil as simply a new part of my relationship with this other family of mine. I am one of the family now, for better or worse: no longer the guest, the exotic American, or the open door to fame in the West. They see my limitations and I see theirs. Painting in Elena's studio day after day, three summers in a row, they now know that I am a sweaty drudge like the rest of them. I can live in Leningrad like them, score an occasional kilo of cheese, get excited by fresh coffee, grow furious at bureaucracy or thrilled by the acquisition of practically anything. Why should I expect concerts?

I feel unusually calm about leaving. None of the usual pangs, tears, yearning wrenches. I figure to be back in the fall—at this point, that seems soon enough. The pervasive sense of depression and pessimism is hard to take. Events in the other republics impinge on us, a spectre of things to come. I will be glad to go home to my friends and my apple tree, to strong morning coffee, easy phone connections, and escapist movies I can understand.

I will be back, though. Like Afrika, who now has the travel-to-America disease, I have to come here every six months or so. I'm not clear why. I don't understand why we Soviets and Americans have to have each other so passionately—perhaps something incomplete in our natures demands fulfillment. Perhaps we can-do Americans need to know that one can live richly without optimism. Perhaps we seek the intensity of life lived close to the bone, although God knows we have many such lives to encounter on our own streets. For me, life in Leningrad is an affirmation that humor, courage, and creativity can be kept alive under the most systematic repression.

Then, too, Soviets make me think. They expect facts and lucid explanations. My first moment of passion for the USSR occurred when a Georgian psychologist asked me what I thought was the goal of therapy. "What is a human being supposed to be?" he challenged me. Slava Afonichev questions the cruel destiny of Russia; Sergei, the nature of leadership; Yul, democracy. This search for lucidity may be part of the great Russian intellectual heritage. Russians like to analyze, to discuss. Americans like to do things. And having been fed only one "truth" by the Soviet media for so many years, Russians are still hungry for outside perspectives. And for art. Art is still vitally important.

I am glad to be made to think about these things; at home I can more easily cruise in silence.

I thrive on the intensity of my friendships here—with Alex, Sergei, Alyona, Elena, Valentin, Yul...the list could go on. We began our acquaintance entangled in snarls of gifts and expectations. They wanted me to help them validate their status as artists, to bring them to America, perhaps to fame and riches; I wanted involvement in something meaningful and creative. In such relationships the question always arises: Wherein lies the friendship and where the usefulness to each other? But I believe we have come to truly love one another.

Our boat rocked toward the mouth of the river between hulking gray naval vessels with odd bulb-like appendages and cranes looming like praying mantises. This is still forbidden territory for foreigners. Alyona wouldn't allow me to take pictures. As our boat neared the Baltic the wind picked up and the waves roughened. From the crest of the chop I thought I spotted the controversial dam. If it is finished it will, theoretically, keep strong east winds from pushing water from the Baltic Sea back up the Neva River. This upriver flow causes flooding in Leningrad every ten years or so. The dam, however, although only half built is already preventing the Baltic from flushing pollutants from the mouth of the river. Some beaches have been closed and new strains of viruses and bacteria proliferate in the stagnating soup. Rumor has it that nine hundred children became seriously infected with meningitis from bathing in the polluted water, but that was hushed up. It will get worse before it gets better.

I feel very sad. I think I have drawn from this city some acceptance of tragedy. Not everything comes out well. Good actions do not necessarily bring good consequences. Commercial success helps neither creativity nor fellowship. Invitations to California have brought everybody pain. Sergei has probably left Alyona for good, but she may keep doing his laundry. Elena may be tempted by stardom and Valentin will carry her luggage. Violence and famine may grow from greater freedom. As the differences between the haves and the have-nots grow, as some can buy food easily through connections while their neighbors stand in fruitless lines, as some can swing trips to the West and others cannot, as rumors of computers and video-cameras in the next apartment proliferate, there will be increasing robberies and muggings. Those who have VCRs turn them off when the television shuts down at midnight so that no one will spot the telltale blue glow through the window. Yul carries mace to protect himself. Everybody fears there will be food riots next winter. And this beautiful river already carries death.

I got a letter a while ago from Yul. "Either it will be good or totally, totally bad," he ended. "I am trying to be optimistic. If in the world there are good people—and I have met many—it means that there is sense in everything, and goodness and love will win out." But at what level?

Maybe I am coming to grips with brown paintings.

Our boat turned into a dark and quiet narrow canal near Alyona's workplace and slipped back in the twilight through the city, past St Isaacs, past the Summer Garden, still and shadowed in the night, and, shooting out once more into the river, crossed it. Landing near the Finland Station, we walked slowly to our train and home to bed.

Photo by Laury Porter

T H E   A U T H O R

Barbara Hazard is an artist living in Berkeley, California. She has taught art in New Haven, Connecticut and in the San Francisco Bay area, and exhibited her paintings and drawings in Chicago, New Haven, San Francisco and Leningrad. She returns to Leningrad for three or four months each year to paint, to exhibit, and to continue her friendships with the artists. In November 1992 she will have a one-woman show in a small museum in St. Petersburg, on Liteiny Boulevard, just off Nevsky Prospekt.

Hazard has an M.A. in Art Therapy from Lone Mountain College. She has three grown children and three granddaughters.